Mastering Prepositions for the TOEFL
(While Building Your Vocabulary)
in Five Minutes a Day

Gail Satter

Copyright and Publishing Information

ISBN: 1453676295
ISBN-13: 9781453676295

INTRODUCTION

Teachers and advanced students know that learning two and three word expressions that include prepositions is painfully difficult. There are two reasons for this difficulty:

     1) There are no rules to help the student with the memorization process and

     2) There are seemingly endless numbers of combinations to be mastered.

Over the years it has become very clear to me that if a student really wants to master these expressions, there is only one way to succeed – he has to study a few of them at a time and then methodically review them. The key to success, I think, is in learning only a few new pieces of information a day – and then reviewing that information for several days.

REVIEW! REVIEW! REVIEW! This is the method on which <u>Mastering Prepositions for TOEFL (While Building Your Vocabulary) In Five Minutes A Day</u> is based.

This book is the compilation of lessons successfully used in my own classroom. In fact, I only put these lessons together as a book because my own students kept asking me to do so. They wanted to have a complete set of the worksheets so that they could frequently and quickly review them whenever they had the chance.

The general format of the book will be instantly clear. Students learn a few expressions each day and then continue to review those expressions while learning new ones.

This book is primarily aimed at the TOEFL/advanced learner. I have intentionally incorporated challenging vocabulary into the text so that the student can improve his reading, listening, and speaking skills at the same time that he is mastering his prepositional expressions.

RECOMMENDATIONS FOR USING THIS BOOK IN CLASS:

1. Weekly Plan

Monday

– Work as a class on the first seven sentences.
– Have one student read each sentence aloud, trying to complete the prepositional expression.
– Have all students repeat each sentence, including the new expression.
– Take time to discuss all new vocabulary, idioms, etc., found in each new sentence.
– Provide synonyms for the words found in the expressions.
– Using the material found in the sentences, ask questions of the students that require them to use the new expressions in sentences.
– Repeat the expressions (not the complete sentences) out loud several times.
– There are seven new expressions a day for students to try. However, many students, especially new students, may be more comfortable attempting only four or five expressions. Students should try to learn the number of expressions that they feel they can master.

Tuesday

– Have students complete the sentences learned on Monday. I often start by having them work alone, but then I have them team up and work together.
– Repeat the format from Monday.

Wednesday

– Have students complete the sentences learned on Tuesday. I often have them work in pairs to come up with new sentences for the expressions learned on Tuesday.
– Have students learn five to seven new expressions.
– Repeat the overall process.

Thursday and Friday

– Have students review the twenty-one learned expressions. Follow the daily format, but look for variety in the review process.
– Discussion questions: Have students talk to each other using the questions at the end of each chapter on either of these days. Teachers should encourage as much conversation as possible.
– Teachers will immediately recognize that I have used informal (and perhaps "lazy") grammar in these questions. I have done this for two reasons. First, I feel it is important to keep the expressions together in their units while they are being learned. Second, most Americans speak in this "lazy" form of English when in informal conversation.

2. The teacher should emphasize oral repetition as much as possible. It is very important that students hear themselves repeat these expressions. It is not important that students repeat the sentences out loud after the first time – in real life students will obviously be using these expressions independent of these exact sentences, so we want them to learn the expressions as independent units.

3. There is a review section after every fourth chapter. Teachers can either assign these review chapters as homework and continue teaching a new unit, or classes can take a full week to review expressions that have already been learned.

4. You will find an answer key at the back of the book. This key also serves as a list of all the expressions found in the book. Whenever possible, answers are given in the simple present tense.

5. Don't prolong this activity. The beauty of the method is that it only takes a few minutes a day. Keep it lively, interesting and BRIEF!

FINAL THOUGHTS

THIS SYSTEM WORKS BECAUSE IT IS STRAIGHTFORWARD AND MANAGEABLE.

STUDENTS SHOULD WORK AT THEIR OWN RATES. If a student finds that he can successfully learn only four expressions a day, than that is the number he should attempt.

REMEMBER: Even a few new expressions every week will slowly add up to a bigger and much improved vocabulary. In my experience, it takes just a few weeks for most students to feel comfortable attempting all seven expressions daily.

Prepositional expressions can be mastered. I know you can do it.

GOOD LUCK AND HAVE FUN!!!

Gail Satter

WEEK 1

MONDAY

1. The teacher never <u>deviates</u> _____ the curriculum.
2. I <u>abstained</u> _____ voting for class president.
3. Are you <u>aware</u> _____ the time? We're very late for the party.
4. John seems very <u>content</u> _____ his job.
5. The grammar book <u>provided</u> us _____ excellent explanations.
6. Amy has a great <u>thirst</u> _____ knowledge.
7. <u>According</u> _____ David, our examination is tomorrow.

TUESDAY

1. The teacher never <u>deviates</u> _____ the curriculum.
2. I <u>abstained</u> _____ voting for class president.
3. Are you <u>aware</u> _____ the time? We're very late for the party.
4. John seems very <u>content</u> _____ his job.
5. The grammar book <u>provided</u> us _____ excellent explanations.
6. Amy has a great <u>thirst</u> _____ knowledge.
7. <u>According</u> _____ David, our examination is tomorrow.
8. I'm so <u>envious</u> _____ Tom's new car. I'm still driving my 1972 Chevy!
9. My sister and mother are always _____ <u>odds</u> _____ each other.
10. I <u>substituted</u> margarine _____ butter in the cake recipe.
11. I <u>contributed</u> two dollars _____ the gift for Elizabeth's birthday.

12. The firefighters <u>rescued</u> fifteen people _____ the burning building.

13. I don't <u>care</u> _____ how I look today because I'm staying home all day.

14. I don't <u>care</u> _____ sausage on my pizza. I prefer vegetables.

WEDNESDAY

1. The teacher never <u>deviates</u> _____ the curriculum.

2. I <u>abstained</u> _____voting for class president.

3. Are you <u>aware</u> _____the time? We're very late for the party.

4. John seems very <u>content</u> _____ his job.

5. The grammar book <u>provided</u> us _____ excellent explanations.

6. Amy has a great <u>thirst</u> _____ knowledge.

7. <u>According</u> _____ David, our examination is tomorrow.

8. I'm so <u>envious</u> _____ Tom's new car. I'm still driving my 1972 Chevy!

9. My sister and mother are always _____ <u>odds</u> _____ each other.

10. I <u>substituted</u> margarine _____butter in the cake recipe.

11. I <u>contributed</u> two dollars _____ the gift for Elizabeth's birthday.

12. The firefighters <u>rescued</u> fifteen people _____ the burning building.

13. I don't <u>care</u> _____ how I look today because I'm staying home all day.

14. I don't <u>care</u> _____ sausage on my pizza. I prefer vegetables.

15. ESL students are on a <u>quest</u> _____ fluency in English.

16. Many teenagers feel that learning math isn't <u>relevant</u> _____ their lives.

17. Paul's opinion on politics completely <u>differs</u> _____ mine.

18. I need to <u>consult</u> _____ a second doctor to confirm my need for surgery.

19. Why do you always <u>side</u> _____ Jimmy instead of with me?

20. I wish you didn't always <u>side</u> _____ me. Can't you ever agree with me?

21. Children with autism are often <u>detached</u> _____ the activities of the world.

THURSDAY

1. The teacher never <u>deviates</u> _____ the curriculum.

2. I <u>abstained</u> _____ voting for class president.

3. Are you <u>aware</u> _____ the time? We're very late for the party.

4. John seems very <u>content</u> _____ his job.

5. The grammar book <u>provided</u> us _____ excellent explanations.

6. Amy has a great <u>thirst</u> _____ knowledge.

7. <u>According</u> _____ David, our examination is tomorrow.

8. I'm so <u>envious</u> _____ Tom's new car. I'm still driving my 1972 Chevy!

9. My sister and mother are always _____ <u>odds</u> _____ each other.

10. I <u>substituted</u> margarine _____ butter in the cake recipe.

11. I <u>contributed</u> two dollars _____ the gift for Elizabeth's birthday.

12. The firefighters <u>rescued</u> fifteen people _____ the burning building.

13. I don't <u>care</u> _____ how I look today because I'm staying home all day.

14. I don't <u>care</u> _____ sausage on my pizza. I prefer vegetables.

15. ESL students are on a <u>quest</u> _____ fluency in English.

16. Many teenagers feel that learning math isn't <u>relevant</u> _____ their lives.

17. Paul's opinion on politics completely <u>differs</u> _____ mine.

18. I need to <u>consult</u> _____ a second doctor to confirm my need for surgery.

19. Why do you always <u>side</u> _____ Jimmy instead of with me?

20. I wish you didn't always <u>side</u> _____ me. Can't you ever agree with me?

21. Children with autism are often <u>detached</u> _____ the activities of the world.

FRIDAY

1. The teacher never <u>deviates</u> _____ the curriculum.

2. I <u>abstained</u> _____ voting for class president.

3. Are you <u>aware</u> _____ the time? We're very late for the party.

4. John seems very <u>content</u> _____ his job.

5. The grammar book <u>provided</u> us _____ excellent explanations.

6. Amy has a great <u>thirst</u> _____ knowledge.

7. <u>According</u> _____ David, our examination is tomorrow.

8. I'm so <u>envious</u> _____ Tom's new car. I'm still driving my 1972 Chevy!

9. My sister and mother are always _____ <u>odds</u> _____ each other.

10. I <u>substituted</u> margarine _____ butter in the cake recipe.

11. I <u>contributed</u> two dollars _____ the gift for Elizabeth's birthday.

12. The firefighters <u>rescued</u> fifteen people _____ the burning building.

13. I don't <u>care</u> _____ how I look today because I'm staying home all day.

14. I don't <u>care</u> _____ sausage on my pizza. I prefer vegetables.

15. ESL students are on a <u>quest</u> _____ fluency in English.

16. Many teenagers feel that learning math isn't <u>relevant</u> _____ their lives.

17. Paul's opinion on politics completely <u>differs</u> _____ mine.

18. I need to <u>consult</u> _____ a second doctor to confirm my need for surgery.

19. Why do you always <u>side</u> _____ Jimmy instead of with me?

20. I wish you didn't always <u>side</u> _____ me. Can't you ever agree with me?

21. Children with autism are often <u>detached</u> _____ the activities of the world.

DISCUSSION

1. Are you <u>content with</u> your current job? What job would you rather have?

2. Name someone you are always <u>at odds with</u>. Why don't you two get along?

3. What's your favorite outfit to wear when you don't <u>care about</u> your appearance? Describe it in detail.

4. Name a food that you really don't <u>care for</u>. Name a food that you passionately love.

5. Describe something about life in your country that <u>differs from</u> life in this country.

WEEK 2

MONDAY

1. _____ the event _____ fire, please leave the room through the exit doors.

2. The jury found Ted Tines innocent _____ all the charges.

3. _____ behalf _____ the decorating committee, I would like to thank you for all of your hard work.

4. Denise excels _____ both sports and painting.

5. When I first came to the United States, I was unfamiliar _____ its language and customs.

6. Children rely _____ their parents for protection.

7. My house is adjacent _____ the school, so my walk is very short each morning.

TUESDAY

1. _____ the event _____ fire, please leave the room through the exit doors.

2. The jury found Ted Tines innocent _____ all the charges.

3. _____ behalf _____ the decorating committee, I would like to thank you for all of your hard work.

4. Denise excels _____ both sports and painting.

5. When I first came to the United States, I was unfamiliar _____ its language and customs.

6. Children <u>rely</u> _____ their parents for protection.

7. My house is <u>adjacent</u> _____ the school, so my walk is very short each morning.

8. Mr. Peters has been <u>blessed</u> _____ great longevity; he just celebrated his 100th birthday.

9. _____ the <u>advice</u> _____ my doctor, I am going to stay home from work next week.

10. Joanna is very <u>homesick</u> _____ her family in Mexico.

11. This class is so <u>crowded</u> _____ students that there isn't even a chair for me!

12. _____ the <u>exception</u> _____ Jonathan, everyone is able to come to the party tonight.

13. In her senior year of high school, Jean got very <u>involved</u> _____ theater.

14. I have an incredible <u>yearning</u> _____ a hot fudge sundae smothered in whipped cream.

WEDNESDAY

1. _____ the <u>event</u> _____ fire, please leave the room through the exit doors.

2. The jury found Ted Tines <u>innocent</u> _____ all the charges.

3. _____ <u>behalf</u> _____ the decorating committee, I would like to thank you for all of your hard work.

4. Denise <u>excels</u> _____ both sports and painting.

5. When I first came to the United States, I was <u>unfamiliar</u> _____ its language and customs.

6. Children <u>rely</u> _____ their parents for protection.

7. My house is <u>adjacent</u> _____ the school, so my walk is very short each morning.

8. Mr. Peters has been <u>blessed</u> _____ great longevity; he just celebrated his 100th birthday.

9. _____ the <u>advice</u> _____ my doctor, I am going to stay home from work next week.

10. Joanna is very <u>homesick</u> _____ her family in Mexico.

11. This class is so <u>crowded</u> _____ students that there isn't even a chair for me!

12. _____ the <u>exception</u> _____ Jonathan, everyone is able to come to the party tonight.

13. In her senior year of high school, Jean got very <u>involved</u> _____ theater.

14. I have an incredible <u>yearning</u> _____ a hot fudge sundae smothered in whipped cream.

15. When you do the wash, remember to <u>separate</u> the dark clothes _____ the light clothes.

16. Mrs. Sanchez is <u>impatient</u> _____ all of her students.

17. Once she <u>emerged</u> _____ her depression, Katy was her happy, spirited self again.

18. I don't know how to <u>deal</u> _____ my mother. She's been so sullen and difficult lately.

19. Little children need to be taught to <u>distinguish</u> _____ right and wrong.

20. The class <u>consists</u> _____ students from over twenty countries.

21. Professor Jameson is an <u>expert</u> _____ nuclear physics.

THURSDAY

1. _____ <u>the event</u> _____ fire, please leave the room through the exit doors.

2. The jury found Ted Tines <u>innocent</u> _____ all the charges.

3. _____ <u>behalf</u> _____ the decorating committee, I would like to thank you for all of your hard work.

4. Denise excels _____ both sports and painting.

5. When I first came to the United States, I was unfamiliar _____ its language and customs.

6. Children rely _____ their parents for protection.

7. My house is adjacent _____the school, so my walk is very short each morning.

8. Mr. Peters has been blessed _____ great longevity; he just celebrated his 100th birthday.

9. _____ the advice _____ my doctor, I am going to stay home from work next week.

10. Joanna is very homesick _____her family in Mexico.

11. This class is so crowded _____ students that there isn't even a chair for me!

12. _____ the exception _____ Jonathan, everyone is able to come to the party tonight.

13. In her senior year of high school, Jean got very involved _____theater.

14. I have an incredible yearning _____ a hot fudge sundae smothered in whipped cream.

15. When you do the wash, remember to separate the dark clothes _____ the light clothes.

16. Mrs. Sanchez is impatient _____ all of her students.

17. Once she emerged _____ her depression, Katy was her happy, spirited self again.

18. I don't know how to deal _____ my mother. She's been so sullen and difficult lately.

19. Little children need to be taught to distinguish _____ right and wrong.

20. The class consists _____ students from over twenty countries.

21. Professor Jameson is an expert _____ nuclear physics.

FRIDAY

1. _____ the event _____ fire, please leave the room through the exit doors.

2. The jury found Ted Tines innocent _____ all the charges.

3. _____ behalf _____ the decorating committee, I would like to thank you for all of your hard work.

4. Denise excels _____ both sports and painting.

5. When I first came to the United States, I was unfamiliar _____ its language and customs.

6. Children rely _____ their parents for protection.

7. My house is adjacent _____the school, so my walk is very short each morning.

8. Mr. Peters has been blessed _____ great longevity; he just celebrated his 100th birthday.

9. _____ the advice _____ my doctor, I am going to stay home from work next week.

10. Joanna is very homesick _____her family in Mexico.

11. This class is so crowded _____ students that there isn't even a chair for me!

12. _____ the exception _____ Jonathan, everyone is able to come to the party tonight.

13. In her senior year of high school, Jean got very involved _____theater.

14. I have an incredible yearning _____ a hot fudge sundae smothered in whipped cream.

15. When you do the wash, remember to separate the dark clothes _____ the light clothes.

16. Mrs. Sanchez is impatient _____ all of her students.

17. Once she <u>emerged</u> _____ her depression, Katy was her happy, spirited self again.

18. I don't know how to <u>deal</u> _____ my mother. She's been so sullen and difficult lately.

19. Little children need to be taught to <u>distinguish</u> _____ right and wrong.

20. The class <u>consists</u> _____ students from over twenty countries.

21. Professor Jameson is an <u>expert</u> _____ nuclear physics.

DISCUSSION

1. Name something you <u>excel at</u>.

2. When you first came to this country and were <u>unfamiliar with</u> absolutely everything, what really "drove you crazy"?

3. What food from home do you <u>frequently yearn for</u>?

4. Are you generally <u>patient with</u> or <u>impatient with</u> people when they make errors or don't understand simple things?

5. How do you <u>deal with</u> mean and nasty people?

WEEK 3

MONDAY

1. My grandfather was completely <u>devoted</u> _____my grandmother.

2. _____ <u>light</u> _____ the evidence, George Smith was convicted of robbing the local bank.

3. I'm <u>responsible</u> _____ bringing dessert to the potluck dinner Friday night.

4. _____ <u>case</u> _____ fire, exit through the doors at the front of the theater.

5. My aunt has <u>disdain</u> _____ everyone who comes from Texas because forty years ago a man from Dallas broke her heart.

6. Why is it that on Monday mornings I am <u>incapable</u> _____ waking up?

7. I can't believe that Mark and Myra are getting married. They are <u>incompatible</u> _____ each other.

TUESDAY

1. My grandfather was completely <u>devoted</u> _____my grandmother.

2. _____ <u>light</u> _____ the evidence, George Smith was convicted of robbing the local bank.

3. I'm <u>responsible</u> _____ bringing dessert to the potluck dinner Friday night.

4. _____ case _____ fire, exit through the doors at the front of the theater.

5. My aunt has <u>disdain</u> _____ everyone who comes from Texas because forty years ago a man from Dallas broke her heart.

6. Why is it that on Monday mornings I am <u>incapable</u> _____ waking up?

7. I can't believe that Mark and Myra are getting married. They are <u>incompatible</u> _____ each other.

8. I'm so <u>tired</u> _____ school that I don't think I can stand studying for one more minute.

9. Toby looks very <u>tired</u> _____ working so hard at the construction site.

10. Poor Mrs. Hidalgo. She's <u>burdened</u> _____ a very ill mother, and she has no siblings to assist her.

11. My mother always <u>blamed</u> me, her oldest child, _____ anything that went wrong in our house.

12. Do you think that I should be <u>concerned</u> _____ my grades in school?

13. When five o'clock comes on Friday, the workers <u>flee</u> _____ their offices as fast as they can.

14. Deborah will never <u>forgive</u> Miguel _____ lying to her.

WEDNESDAY

1. My grandfather was completely <u>devoted</u> _____ my grandmother.

2. _____ <u>light</u> _____ the evidence, George Smith was convicted of robbing the local bank.

3. I'm <u>responsible</u> _____ bringing dessert to the potluck dinner Friday night.

4. _____ case _____ fire, exit through the doors at the front of the theater.

5. My aunt has disdain _____ everyone who comes from Texas because forty years ago a man from Dallas broke her heart.

6. Why is it that on Monday mornings I am incapable _____ waking up?

7. I can't believe that Mark and Myra are getting married. They are incompatible _____ each other.

8. I'm so tired _____ school that I don't think I can stand studying for one more minute.

9. Toby looks very tired _____ working so hard at the construction site.

10. Poor Mrs. Hidalgo. She's burdened _____ a very ill mother, and she has no siblings to assist her.

11. My mother always blamed me, her oldest child, _____ anything that went wrong in our house.

12. Do you think that I should be concerned _____ my grades in school?

13. When five o'clock comes on Friday, the workers flee _____ their offices as fast as they can.

14. Deborah will never forgive Miguel _____ lying to her.

15. In your country, are you free to dissent _____ your government's politics?

16. Remember to be polite _____ Mr. Talino even though you can't stand him.

17. The protesters are demonstrating _____ the company's failure to give them a raise.

18. I am so bored _____ my job that I could scream! It's really time to start pounding the pavement.

19. Whenever I'm sad, I can <u>count</u> _____ my friend Patricia to make me laugh.

20. Judith was at the <u>zenith</u> _____ her career when she decided to "chuck it all," retire, and travel around the world.

21. It took me a week to <u>respond</u> _____ my mother's letter. I was just swamped with work.

THURSDAY

1. My grandfather was completely <u>devoted</u> _____my grandmother.

2. _____ <u>light</u> _____ the evidence, George Smith was convicted of robbing the local bank.

3. I'm <u>responsible</u> _____ bringing dessert to the potluck dinner Friday night.

4. _____ <u>case</u> _____ fire, exit through the doors at the front of the theater.

5. My aunt has <u>disdain</u> _____ everyone who comes from Texas because forty years ago a man from Dallas broke her heart.

6. Why is it that on Monday mornings I am <u>incapable</u> _____ waking up?

7. I can't believe that Mark and Myra are getting married. They are <u>incompatible</u> _____ each other.

8. I'm so <u>tired</u> _____ school that I don't think I can stand studying for one more minute.

9. Toby looks very <u>tired</u> _____ working so hard at the construction site.

10. Poor Mrs. Hidalgo. She's <u>burdened</u> _____ a very ill mother, and she has no siblings to assist her.

11. My mother always <u>blamed</u> me, her oldest child, _____ anything that went wrong in our house.

12. Do you think that I should be <u>concerned</u> _____ my grades in school?

13. When five o'clock comes on Friday, the workers <u>flee</u> _____ their offices as fast as they can.

14. Deborah will never <u>forgive</u> Miguel _____ lying to her.

15. In your country, are you free to <u>dissent</u> _____ your government's politics?

16. Remember to be <u>polite</u> _____ Mr. Talino even though you can't stand him.

17. The protesters are <u>demonstrating</u> _____ the company's failure to give them a raise.

18. I am so <u>bored</u> _____ my job that I could scream! It's really time to start pounding the pavement.

19. Whenever I'm sad, I can <u>count</u> _____ my friend Patricia to make me laugh.

20. Judith was at the <u>zenith</u> _____ her career when she decided to "chuck it all," retire, and travel around the world.

21. It took me a week to <u>respond</u> _____ my mother's letter. I was just swamped with work.

FRIDAY

1. My grandfather was completely <u>devoted</u> _____ my grandmother.

2. _____ <u>light</u> _____ the evidence, George Smith was convicted of robbing the local bank.

3. I'm <u>responsible</u> _____ bringing dessert to the potluck dinner Friday night.

4. _____ case _____ fire, exit through the doors at the front of the theater.

5. My aunt has <u>disdain</u> _____ everyone who comes from Texas because forty years ago a man from Dallas broke her heart.

6. Why is it that on Monday mornings I am <u>incapable</u> _____ waking up?

7. I can't believe that Mark and Myra are getting married. They are <u>incompatible</u> _____ each other.

8. I'm so <u>tired</u> _____ school that I don't think I can stand studying for one more minute.

9. Toby looks very <u>tired</u> _____ working so hard at the construction site.

10. Poor Mrs. Hidalgo. She's <u>burdened</u> _____ a very ill mother, and she has no siblings to assist her.

11. My mother always <u>blamed</u> me, her oldest child, _____ anything that went wrong in our house.

12. Do you think that I should be <u>concerned</u> _____ my grades in school?

13. When five o'clock comes on Friday, the workers <u>flee</u> _____ their offices as fast as they can.

14. Deborah will never <u>forgive</u> Miguel _____ lying to her.

15. In your country, are you free to <u>dissent</u> _____ your government's politics?

16. Remember to be <u>polite</u> _____ Mr. Talino even though you can't stand him.

17. The protesters are <u>demonstrating</u> _____ the company's failure to give them a raise.

18. I am so <u>bored</u> _____ my job that I could scream! It's really time to start pounding the pavement.

19. Whenever I'm sad, I can <u>count</u> _____ my friend Patricia to make me laugh.

20. Judith was at the <u>zenith</u> _____ her career when she decided to "chuck it all," retire, and travel around the world.

21. It took me a week to <u>respond</u> _____ my mother's letter. I was just swamped with work.

DISCUSSION

1. Name something that you are <u>tired of</u> doing but that you must continue doing. (I know it's not coming to English class!!!)

2. Could you <u>forgive</u> someone you loved <u>for</u> "cheating on" you? Could you continue the relationship?

3. In your country, is <u>dissent from</u> the government permitted? Are there limits to the dissent that is permitted?

4. Name three things- beliefs, values, items, animals- that your are <u>devoted to</u>? Now name the people <u>to</u> whom you are <u>devoted</u>.

5. What two things are you most <u>concerned about</u> right now? (What do you worry about at night when you should be sleeping?)

WEEK 4

MONDAY

1. Let's <u>take</u> <u>advantage</u> _____the restaurant's Early Bird Special. If we eat at 5 o'clock, a complete dinner will only cost $5.00.

2. My goal is to be <u>proficient</u> _____ Spanish by the end of the year. Then I'll continue studying to get really good at it.

3. Jonathan has a really negative <u>attitude</u> _____ school: he never does his homework.

4. Do you think there's a <u>connection</u> _____ my eating too many ice cream sundaes and my recent weight gain?

5. _____ a little <u>help</u> _____ my friends, I finally finished painting the house.

6. Pumpkins, corn, and tomatoes are three examples of foods that are <u>indigenous</u> _____ North and South America. What foods are native to your country?

7. Tammy was <u>annoyed</u> _____ her teacher for giving such a difficult examination.

TUESDAY

1. Let's <u>take</u> <u>advantage</u> _____the restaurant's Early Bird Special. If we eat at 5 o'clock, a complete dinner will only cost $5.00.

2. My goal is to be <u>proficient</u> _____ Spanish by the end of the year. Then I'll continue studying to get really good at it.

3. Jonathan has a really negative <u>attitude</u> _____ school: he never does his homework.

4. Do you think there's a <u>connection</u> _____ my eating too many ice cream sundaes and my recent weight gain?

5. _____ a little <u>help</u> _____ my friends, I finally finished painting the house.

6. Pumpkins, corn, and tomatoes are three examples of foods that are <u>indigenous</u> _____ North and South America. What foods are native to your country?

7. Tammy was <u>annoyed</u> _____ her teacher for giving such a difficult examination.

8. John was <u>annoyed</u> _____ his grade; he thought he deserved a higher score on the test.

9. What would you <u>wish</u> _____ if a magic genie gave you three free wishes?

10. When teenagers suddenly offer to clean their rooms and help with the housework, mothers are very <u>suspicious</u> _____ their motivations.

11. During dinner last night, David and Paula had a <u>quarrel</u> _____ each other.

12. They were angrily <u>quarreling</u> _____ whose night it was to wash the dishes. Silly, isn't it?

13. Tony and Marissa spent the afternoon looking at <u>photographs</u> _____ their wedding reception.

14. _____ <u>second thought</u>, let's not go out tonight. Let's have a cozy night at home.

WEDNESDAY

1. Let's <u>take</u> <u>advantage</u> _____ the restaurant's Early Bird Special. If we eat at 5 o'clock, a complete dinner will only cost $5.00.

2. My goal is to be <u>proficient</u> _____ Spanish by the end of the year. Then I'll continue studying to get really good at it.

3. Jonathan has a really negative <u>attitude</u> _____ school: he never does his homework.

4. Do you think there's a <u>connection</u> _____ my eating too many ice cream sundaes and my recent weight gain?

5. _____ a little <u>help</u> _____ my friends, I finally finished painting the house.

6. Pumpkins, corn, and tomatoes are three examples of foods that are <u>indigenous</u> _____ North and South America. What foods are native to your country?

7. Tammy was <u>annoyed</u> _____ her teacher for giving such a difficult examination.

8. John was <u>annoyed</u> _____ his grade; he thought he deserved a higher score on the test.

9. What would you <u>wish</u> _____ if a magic genie gave you three free wishes?

10. When teenagers suddenly offer to clean their rooms and help with the housework, mothers are very <u>suspicious</u> _____ their motivations.

11. During dinner last night, David and Paula had a <u>quarrel</u> _____ each other.

12. They were angrily <u>quarreling</u> _____ whose night it was to wash the dishes. Silly, isn't it?

13. Tony and Marissa spent the afternoon looking at <u>photographs</u> _____ their wedding reception.

14. _____ <u>second thought</u>, let's not go out tonight. Let's have a cozy night at home.

15. The elderly spend many hours <u>looking back</u> _____ their younger years.

16. Why does your mother <u>object</u> _____ every girl you date?

17. Let's go shopping for food tomorrow. _____ the meantime, though, let's order a pizza.

18. My boss always digresses _____ the agendas set for our meetings, so they last for hours and hours.

19. My English teacher often confuses me _____ my cousin Pedro.

20. I am confused _____ tenses. No matter how long I study, I still can't master the future tenses.

21. Jessica was so engrossed _____ her novel that she didn't hear the telephone ring, even though it rang twenty-two times!

THURSDAY

1. Let's take advantage _____ the restaurant's Early Bird Special. If we eat at 5 o'clock, a complete dinner will only cost $5.00.

2. My goal is to be proficient _____ Spanish by the end of the year. Then I'll continue studying to get really good at it.

3. Jonathan has a really negative attitude _____ school: he never does his homework.

4. Do you think there's a connection _____ my eating too many ice cream sundaes and my recent weight gain?

5. _____ a little help _____ my friends, I finally finished painting the house.

6. Pumpkins, corn, and tomatoes are three examples of foods that are indigenous _____ North and South America. What foods are native to your country?

7. Tammy was annoyed _____ her teacher for giving such a difficult examination.

8. John was annoyed _____ his grade; he thought he deserved a higher score on the test.

9. What would you wish _____ if a magic genie gave you three free wishes?

10. When teenagers suddenly offer to clean their rooms and help with the housework, mothers are very suspicious _____ their motivations.

11. During dinner last night, David and Paula had a quarrel _____ each other.

12. They were angrily quarreling _____ whose night it was to wash the dishes. Silly, isn't it?

13. Tony and Marissa spent the afternoon looking at photographs _____ their wedding reception.

14. _____ second thought, let's not go out tonight. Let's have a cozy night at home.

15. The elderly spend many hours looking back _____ their younger years.

16. Why does your mother object _____ every girl you date?

17. Let's go shopping for food tomorrow. _____ the meantime, though, let's order a pizza.

18. My boss always digresses _____ the agendas set for our meetings, so they last for hours and hours.

19. My English teacher often confuses me _____my cousin Pedro.

20. I am confused _____ tenses. No matter how long I study, I still can't master the future tenses.

21. Jessica was so engrossed _____ her novel that she didn't hear the telephone ring, even though it rang twenty-two times!

FRIDAY

1. Let's take advantage _____the restaurant's Early Bird Special. If we eat at 5 o'clock, a complete dinner will only cost $5.00.

2. My goal is to be <u>proficient</u> _____ Spanish by the end of the year. Then I'll continue studying to get really good at it.

3. Jonathan has a really negative <u>attitude</u> _____ school: he never does his homework.

4. Do you think there's a <u>connection</u> _____ my eating too many ice cream sundaes and my recent weight gain?

5. _____ a little <u>help</u> _____ my friends, I finally finished painting the house.

6. Pumpkins, corn, and tomatoes are three examples of foods that are <u>indigenous</u> _____ North and South America. What foods are native to your country?

7. Tammy was <u>annoyed</u> _____ her teacher for giving such a difficult examination.

8. John was <u>annoyed</u> _____ his grade; he thought he deserved a higher score on the test.

9. What would you <u>wish</u> _____ if a magic genie gave you three free wishes?

10. When teenagers suddenly offer to clean their rooms and help with the housework, mothers are very <u>suspicious</u> _____ their motivations.

11. During dinner last night, David and Paula had a <u>quarrel</u> _____ each other.

12. They were angrily <u>quarreling</u> _____ whose night it was to wash the dishes. Silly, isn't it?

13. Tony and Marissa spent the afternoon looking at <u>photographs</u> _____ their wedding reception.

14. _____ <u>second thought</u>, let's not go out tonight, Let's have a cozy night at home.

15. The elderly spend many hours <u>looking back</u> _____ their younger years.

16. Why does your mother <u>object</u> _____ every girl you date?

17. Let's go shopping for food tomorrow. _____ <u>the meantime,</u> though, let's order a pizza.

18. My boss always digresses _____ the agendas set for our meetings, so they last for hours and hours.

19. My English teacher often <u>confuses</u> me _____my cousin Pedro.

20. I am <u>confused</u> _____ tenses. No matter how long I study, I still can't master the future tenses.

21. Jessica was so <u>engrossed</u> _____ her novel that she didn't hear the telephone ring, even though it rang twenty-two times!

DISCUSSION

1. Name something you are <u>proficient at</u>.

2. Name a food that is <u>indigenous to</u> your country. Name a food that is not <u>indigenous to</u> your county.

3. What would you <u>wish for</u> if a magic genie gave you three free wishes?

4. Whom was your last <u>quarrel with</u>? What did you <u>quarrel about</u>?

5. <u>Look back on</u> your childhood and tell your partner about a really happy memory.

REVIEW WEEKS 1-4

WEEK 1

1. The teacher never <u>deviates</u> _____ the curriculum.

2. I <u>abstained</u> _____ voting for class president.

3. Are you <u>aware</u> _____ the time? We're very late for the party.

4. John seems very <u>content</u> _____ his job.

5. The grammar book <u>provided</u> us _____ excellent explanations.

6. Amy has a great <u>thirst</u> _____ knowledge.

7. <u>According</u> _____ David, our examination is tomorrow.

8. I'm so <u>envious</u> _____ Tom's new car. I'm still driving my 1972 Chevy!

9. My sister and mother are always _____ <u>odds</u> _____ each other.

10. I <u>substituted</u> margarine _____ butter in the cake recipe.

11. I <u>contributed</u> two dollars _____ the gift for Elizabeth's birthday.

12. The firefighters <u>rescued</u> fifteen people _____ the burning building.

13. I don't <u>care</u> _____ how I look today because I'm staying home all day.

14. I don't <u>care</u> _____ sausage on my pizza. I prefer vegetables.

15. ESL students are on a <u>quest</u> _____ fluency in English.

16. Many teenagers feel that learning math isn't <u>relevant</u> _____ their lives.

17. Paul's opinion on politics completely <u>differs</u> _____ mine.

18. I need to <u>consult</u> _____ a second doctor to confirm my need for surgery.

19. Why do you always <u>side</u> _____ Jimmy instead of with me?

20. I wish you didn't always <u>side</u> _____ me. Can't you ever agree with me?

21. Children with autism are often <u>detached</u> _____ the activities of the world.

WEEK 2

1. _____ the <u>event</u> _____ fire, please leave the room through the exit doors.

2. The jury found Ted Tines <u>innocent</u> _____ all the charges.

3. _____ <u>behalf</u> _____ the decorating committee, I would like to thank you for all of your hard work.

4. Denise <u>excels</u> _____ both sports and painting.

5. When I first came to the United States, I was <u>unfamiliar</u> _____ its language and customs.

6. Children <u>rely</u> _____ their parents for protection.

7. My house is <u>adjacent</u> _____the school, so my walk is very short each morning.

8. Mr. Peters has been <u>blessed</u> _____ great longevity; he just celebrated his 100th birthday.

9. _____ the <u>advice</u> _____ my doctor, I am going to stay home from work next week.

10. Joanna is very <u>homesick</u> _____her family in Mexico.

11. This class is so <u>crowded</u> _____ students that there isn't even a chair for me!

12. _____ the <u>exception</u> _____ Jonathan, everyone is able to come to the party tonight.

13. In her senior year of high school, Jean got very <u>involved</u> _____ theater.

14. I have an incredible <u>yearning</u> _____ a hot fudge sundae smothered in whipped cream.

15. When you do the wash, remember to <u>separate</u> the dark clothes _____ the light clothes.

16. Mrs. Sanchez is <u>impatient</u> _____ all of her students.

17. Once she <u>emerged</u> _____ her depression, Katy was her happy, spirited self again.

18. I don't know how to <u>deal</u> _____ my mother. She's been so sullen and difficult lately.

19. Little children need to be taught to <u>distinguish</u> _____ right and wrong.

20. The class <u>consists</u> _____ students from over twenty countries.

21. Professor Jameson is an <u>expert</u> _____ nuclear physics.

WEEK 3

1. My grandfather was completely <u>devoted</u> _____my grandmother.

2. _____ <u>light</u> _____ the evidence, George Smith was convicted of robbing the local bank.

3. I'm <u>responsible</u> _____ bringing dessert to the potluck dinner Friday night.

4. _____ <u>case</u> _____ fire, exit through the doors at the front of the theater.

5. My aunt has <u>disdain</u> _____ everyone who comes from Texas because forty years ago a man from Dallas broke her heart.

6. Why is it that on Monday mornings I am <u>incapable</u> _____ waking up?

7. I can't believe that Mark and Myra are getting married. They are incompatible _____ each other.

8. I'm so tired _____ school that I don't think I can stand studying for one more minute.

9. Toby looks very tired _____ working so hard at the construction site.

10. Poor Mrs. Hidalgo. She's burdened _____ a very ill mother, and she has no siblings to assist her.

11. My mother always blamed me, her oldest child, _____ anything that went wrong in our house.

12. Do you think that I should be concerned _____ my grades in school?

13. When five o'clock comes on Friday, the workers flee _____ their offices as fast as they can.

14. Deborah will never forgive Miguel _____ lying to her.

15. In your country, are you free to dissent _____ your government's politics?

16. Remember to be polite _____ Mr. Talino even though you can't stand him.

17. The protesters are demonstrating _____ the company's failure to give them a raise.

18. I am so bored _____ my job that I could scream! It's really time to start pounding the pavement.

19. Whenever I'm sad, I can count _____ my friend Patricia to make me laugh.

20. Judith was at the zenith _____ her career when she decided to "chuck it all," retire, and travel around the world.

21. It took me a week to respond _____ my mother's letter. I was just swamped with work.

WEEK 4

1. Let's <u>take</u> <u>advantage</u> _____ the restaurant's Early Bird Special. If we eat at 5 o'clock, a complete dinner will only cost $5.00.

2. My goal is to be <u>proficient</u> _____ Spanish by the end of the year. Then I'll continue studying to get really good at it.

3. Jonathan has a really negative <u>attitude</u> _____ school: he never does his homework.

4. Do you think there's a <u>connection</u> _____ my eating too many ice cream sundaes and my recent weight gain?

5. _____ a little <u>help</u> _____ my friends, I finally finished painting the house.

6. Pumpkins, corn, and tomatoes are three examples of foods that are <u>indigenous</u> _____ North and South America. What foods are native to your country?

7. Tammy was <u>annoyed</u> _____ her teacher for giving such a difficult examination.

8. John was <u>annoyed</u> _____ his grade; he thought he deserved a higher score on the test.

9. What would you <u>wish</u> _____ if a magic genie gave you three free wishes?

10. When teenagers suddenly offer to clean their rooms and help with the housework, mothers are very <u>suspicious</u> _____ their motivations.

11. During dinner last night, David and Paula had a <u>quarrel</u> _____ each other.

12. They were angrily <u>quarreling</u> _____ whose night it was to wash the dishes. Silly, isn't it?

13. Tony and Marissa spent the afternoon looking at <u>photographs</u> _____ their wedding reception.

14. _____ second thought, let's not go out tonight. Let's have a cozy night at home.

15. The elderly spend many hours looking back _____ their younger years.

16. Why does your mother object _____ every girl you date?

17. Let's go shopping for food tomorrow. _____ the meantime, though, let's order a pizza.

18. My boss always digresses _____ the agendas set for our meetings, so they last for hours and hours.

19. My English teacher often confuses me _____ my cousin Pedro.

20. I am confused _____ tenses. No matter how long I study, I still can't master the future tenses.

21. Jessica was so engrossed _____ her novel that she didn't hear the telephone ring, even though it rang twenty-two times!

WEEK 5

MONDAY

1. Mr. Potter was always very <u>kind</u> _____ the children who lived in his neighborhood.

2. It was very <u>kind</u> _____ Mr. Potter to invite the children over to watch a movie at his house last Saturday.

3. Paula had to miss dance class yesterday <u>because</u> _____ her bad back.

4. The thieves <u>held</u> _____ the grocery store, stealing over $500.

5. _____ <u>retrospect</u>, I can't believe I turned Juan down when he asked me to marry him. What a mistake I made!

6. Many hours of studying <u>resulted</u> _____ my getting an "A" on the final examination.

7. An "A" on the final examination was <u>the result</u> _____ many hours of studying.

TUESDAY

1. Mr. Potter was always very <u>kind</u> _____ the children who lived in his neighborhood.

2. It was very <u>kind</u> _____ Mr. Potter to invite the children over to watch a movie at his house last Saturday.

3. Paula had to miss dance class yesterday <u>because</u> _____ her bad back.

4. The thieves <u>held</u> _____ the grocery store, stealing over $500.

5. _____ retrospect, I can't believe I turned Juan down when he asked me to marry him. What a mistake I made!

6. Many hours of studying resulted _____ my getting an "A" on the final examination.

7. An "A" on the final examination was the result _____ many hours of studying.

8. Toshiko always smiles _____ her customers.

9. I'm going to exercise in the park tomorrow regardless _____ the weather.

10. Would it be possible _____ you to give me a ride to class tomorrow night?

11. Let's plan _____ going to a movie this Saturday night.

12. Every once _____ a while it's fun to spend the entire after-noon gardening in my yard.

13. The picnic was canceled _____ account _____ bad weather.

14. When you were a teenager, did you always listen _____ your parents?

WEDNESDAY

1. Mr. Potter was always very kind _____ the children who lived in his neighborhood.

2. It was very kind _____ Mr. Potter to invite the children over to watch a movie at his house last Saturday.

3. Paula had to miss dance class yesterday because _____ her bad back.

4. The thieves held _____ the grocery store, stealing over $500.

5. _____ retrospect, I can't believe I turned Juan down when he asked me to marry him. What a mistake I made!

6. Many hours of studying <u>resulted</u> _____ my getting an "A" on the final examination.

7. An "A" on the final examination was <u>the result</u> _____ many hours of studying.

8. Toshiko always <u>smiles</u> _____ her customers.

9. I'm going to exercise in the park tomorrow <u>regardless</u> _____ the weather.

10. Would it be <u>possible</u> _____ you to give me a ride to class tomorrow night?

11. Let's <u>plan</u> _____ going to a movie this Saturday night.

12. Every <u>once</u> _____ <u>a while</u> it's fun to spend the entire after-noon gardening in my yard.

13. The picnic was canceled _____ <u>account</u> _____ bad weather.

14. When you were a teenager, did you always <u>listen</u> _____ your parents?

15. Mrs. Seeger is such a worry-wart! She <u>worries</u> _____ everything.

16. I don't want to <u>work</u> _____ Mayumi on the class project because she never completes her work on time.

17. The English teacher can't <u>account</u> _____ five of her class grammar books. Where could they have gone?

18. It's very difficult to get <u>accustomed</u> _____ the customs of a new country.

19. <u>As a result</u> _____ yesterday's election, Tony is the new presi-dent of the school.

20. Mrs. Garcia is <u>resigned</u> _____ studying day and night this year for her TOEFL exam. She knows that she must do well on it, so she has made up her mind to give it her best shot.

21. Let's <u>take a chance</u> _____ the new pizzeria that just opened. Okay?

THURSDAY

1. Mr. Potter was always very <u>kind</u> _____ the children who lived in his neighborhood.

2. It was very <u>kind</u> _____ Mr. Potter to invite the children over to watch a movie at his house last Saturday.

3. Paula had to miss dance class yesterday <u>because</u> _____ her bad back.

4. The thieves <u>held</u> _____ the grocery store, stealing over $500.

5. _____ <u>retrospect</u>, I can't believe I turned Juan down when he asked me to marry him. What a mistake I made!

6. Many hours of studying <u>resulted</u> _____ my getting an "A" on the final examination.

7. An "A" on the final examination was <u>the result</u> _____ many hours of studying.

8. Toshiko always <u>smiles</u> _____ her customers.

9. I'm going to exercise in the park tomorrow <u>regardless</u> _____ the weather.

10. Would it be <u>possible</u> _____ you to give me a ride to class tomorrow night?

11. Let's <u>plan</u> _____ going to a movie this Saturday night.

12. Every <u>once</u> _____ <u>a while</u> it's fun to spend the entire afternoon gardening in my yard.

13. The picnic was canceled _____ <u>account</u> _____ bad weather.

14. When you were a teenager, did you always <u>listen</u> _____ your parents?

15. Mrs. Seeger is such a worry-wart! She <u>worries</u> _____ everything.

16. I don't want to <u>work</u> _____ Mayumi on the class project because she never completes her work on time.

17. The English teacher can't <u>account</u> _____ five of her class grammar books. Where could they have gone?

18. It's very difficult to get <u>accustomed</u> _____ the customs of a new country.

19. <u>As a result</u> _____ yesterday's election, Tony is the new president of the school.

20. Mrs. Garcia is <u>resigned</u> _____ studying day and night this year for her TOEFL exam. She knows that she must do well on it, so she has made up her mind to give it her best shot.

21. Let's <u>take a chance</u> _____ the new pizzeria that just opened. Okay?

FRIDAY

1. Mr. Potter was always very <u>kind</u> _____ the children who lived in his neighborhood.

2. It was very <u>kind</u> _____ Mr. Potter to invite the children over to watch a movie at his house last Saturday.

3. Paula had to miss dance class yesterday <u>because</u> _____ her bad back.

4. The thieves <u>held</u> _____ the grocery store, stealing over $500.

5. _____ <u>retrospect</u>, I can't believe I turned Juan down when he asked me to marry him. What a mistake I made!

6. Many hours of studying <u>resulted</u> _____ my getting an "A" on the final examination.

7. An "A" on the final examination was <u>the result</u> _____ many hours of studying.

8. Toshiko always <u>smiles</u> _____ her customers.

9. I'm going to exercise in the park tomorrow <u>regardless</u> _____ the weather.

10. Would it be <u>possible</u> _____ you to give me a ride to class tomorrow night?

11. Let's <u>plan</u> _____ going to a movie this Saturday night.

12. Every <u>once</u> _____ <u>a while</u> it's fun to spend the entire after-noon gardening in my yard.

13. The picnic was canceled _____ <u>account</u> _____ bad weather.

14. When you were a teenager, did you always <u>listen</u> _____ your parents?

15. Mrs. Seeger is such a worry-wart! She <u>worries</u> _____ everything.

16. I don't want to <u>work</u> _____ Mayumi on the class project because she never completes her work on time.

17. The English teacher can't <u>account</u> _____ five of her class grammar books. Where could they have gone?

18. It's very difficult to get <u>accustomed</u> _____ the customs of a new country.

19. <u>As a result</u> _____ yesterday's election, Tony is the new presi-dent of the school.

20. Mrs. Garcia is <u>resigned</u> _____ studying day and night this year for her TOEFL exam. She knows that she must do well on it, so she has made up her mind to give it her best shot.

21. Let's <u>take a chance</u> _____ the new pizzeria that just opened. Okay?

DISCUSSION

1. In your culture, do strangers <u>smile at</u> each other when they pass on the street?

2. Do you like to <u>take chances on</u> new things, or do you prefer to stay with the "tried and true"?

3. Do you tend to <u>worry about</u> things? Are you a "worry-wart"?

4. Do you think that it is <u>possible</u> or <u>impossible for</u> there to be life on other planets? Are we alone in the universe?

5. Name something that your parents were absolutely right about — some piece of advice that you wish you had <u>listened to</u>.

WEEK 6

MONDAY

1. Jonas was <u>doubtful</u> _____ his decision to fly east to attend his cousin's wedding. The flight was just too expensive.

2. _____ <u>times</u> I dream of dropping everything and moving to Tahiti.

3. Benjamin and I went out on our first date last night, but we had nothing _____ <u>common</u>.

4. How old were you when you stopped <u>believing</u> _____ Santa Claus?

5. The tag says that this sleeping bag is <u>suitable</u> _____ weather conditions as cold as 0 degrees centigrade.

6. Paul quickly <u>succumbed</u> _____ Peggy's quirky, funny personality and fell head over heels in love with her.

7. _____ <u>the</u> <u>time</u> <u>being</u>, John is working as a substitute teacher. He hopes that a full-time job will become available soon.

TUESDAY

1. Jonas was <u>doubtful</u> _____ his decision to fly east to attend his cousin's wedding. The flight was just too expensive.

2. _____ <u>times</u> I dream of dropping everything and moving to Tahiti.

3. Benjamin and I went out on our first date last night, but we had nothing _____ <u>common</u>.

4. How old were you when you stopped <u>believing</u> _____ Santa Claus?

5. The tag says that this sleeping bag is <u>suitable</u> _____ weather conditions as cold as 0 degrees centigrade.

6. Paul quickly <u>succumbed</u> _____ Peggy's quirky, funny personality and fell head over heels in love with her.

7. _____ the <u>time being</u>, John is working as a substitute teacher. He hopes that a full-time job will become available soon.

8. <u>First</u> _____ <u>all</u>, never cross the street without looking in both directions.

9. Tina <u>called</u> _____ her wedding just hours before the ceremony.

10. Never let Gustavo <u>borrow</u> money _____ you; you'll never see it again!

11. <u>All</u> _____ <u>all</u>, it was a fabulous party!

12. Don't you <u>long</u> _____ the day that little robots will do all of our household chores?

13. Even though I know that there is no <u>use</u> _____ worrying, I sometimes lie awake at night contemplating awful things that might happen.

14. My teacher's explanations are long and unclear. I wish she'd just <u>come</u> _____ the point!

WEDNESDAY

1. Jonas was <u>doubtful</u> _____ his decision to fly east to attend his cousin's wedding. The flight was just too expensive.

2. _____ <u>times</u> I dream of dropping everything and moving to Tahiti.

3. Benjamin and I went out on our first date last night, but we had nothing _____ <u>common</u>.

4. How old were you when you stopped <u>believing</u> _____ Santa Claus?

5. The tag says that this sleeping bag is <u>suitable</u> _____ weather conditions as cold as 0 degrees centigrade.

6. Paul quickly <u>succumbed</u> _____ Peggy's quirky, funny personality and fell head over heels in love with her.

7. _____ the <u>time</u> <u>being</u>, John is working as a substitute teacher. He hopes that a full-time job will become available soon.

8. <u>First</u> _____ <u>all</u>, never cross the street without looking in both directions.

9. Tina <u>called</u> _____ her wedding just hours before the ceremony.

10. Never let Gustavo <u>borrow</u> money _____ you; you'll never see it again!

11. <u>All</u> _____ <u>all</u>, it was a fabulous party!

12. Don't you <u>long</u> _____ the day that little robots will do all of our household chores?

13. Even though I know that there is no <u>use</u> _____ worrying, I sometimes lie awake at night contemplating awful things that might happen.

14. My teacher's explanations are long and unclear. I wish she'd just <u>come</u> _____ the point!

15. My family usually eats at home, but _____ <u>occasion</u>, we treat ourselves to a meal at a restaurant.

16. Because many parents don't <u>approve</u> _____ tattoos, teens often don't tell them when they get one.

17. Anton is very <u>generous</u> _____ his car. He has allowed me to borrow it several times when I desperately needed transportation.

18. The wind was blowing with such force that it nearly <u>knocked</u> me _____ when I crossed the street.

19. Blue jeans <u>shrink</u> _____ hot water.

20. One of the <u>causes</u> _____ the American Civil War was slavery.

21. I just received an e-mail from Samantha. I can't wait to <u>reply</u> _____ her.

THURSDAY

1. Jonas was <u>doubtful</u> _____ his decision to fly east to attend his cousin's wedding. The flight was just too expensive.

2. _____ <u>times</u> I dream of dropping everything and moving to Tahiti.

3. Benjamin and I went out on our first date last night, but we had nothing _____ <u>common</u>.

4. How old were you when you stopped <u>believing</u> _____ Santa Claus?

5. The tag says that this sleeping bag is <u>suitable</u> _____ weather conditions as cold as 0 degrees centigrade.

6. Paul quickly <u>succumbed</u> _____ Peggy's quirky, funny personality and fell head over heels in love with her.

7. _____ the <u>time</u> <u>being</u>, John is working as a substitute teacher. He hopes that a full-time job will become available soon.

8. <u>First</u> _____ <u>all</u>, never cross the street without looking in both directions.

9. Tina <u>called</u> _____ her wedding just hours before the ceremony.

10. Never let Gustavo <u>borrow</u> money _____ you; you'll never see it again!

11. <u>All</u> _____ <u>all</u>, it was a fabulous party!

12. Don't you <u>long</u> _____ the day that little robots will do all of our household chores?

13. Even though I know that there is no <u>use</u> _____worrying, I sometimes lie awake at night contemplating awful things that might happen.

14. My teacher's explanations are long and unclear. I wish she'd just <u>come</u> _____ the point!

15. My family usually eats at home, but _____ <u>occasion</u>, we treat ourselves to a meal at a restaurant.

16. Because many parents don't <u>approve</u> _____ tattoos, teens often don't tell them when they get one.

17. Anton is very <u>generous</u> _____ his car. He has allowed me to borrow it several times when I desperately needed transportation.

18. The wind was blowing with such force that it nearly <u>knocked</u> me _____ when I crossed the street.

19. Blue jeans <u>shrink</u> _____ hot water.

20. One of the <u>causes</u> _____ the American Civil War was slavery.

21. I just received an e-mail from Samantha. I can't wait to <u>reply</u> _____ her.

FRIDAY

1. Jonas was <u>doubtful</u> _____ his decision to fly east to attend his cousin's wedding. The flight was just too expensive.

2. _____ <u>times</u> I dream of dropping everything and moving to Tahiti.

3. Benjamin and I went out on our first date last night, but we had nothing _____ <u>common</u>.

4. How old were you when you stopped <u>believing</u> _____ Santa Claus?

5. The tag says that this sleeping bag is <u>suitable</u> _____ weather conditions as cold as 0 degrees centigrade.

6. Paul quickly <u>succumbed</u> _____ Peggy's quirky, funny personality and fell head over heels in love with her.

7. _____ the <u>time</u> <u>being</u>, John is working as a substitute teacher.
He hopes that a full-time job will become available soon.

8. <u>First</u> _____ <u>all</u>, never cross the street without looking in both
directions.

9. Tina <u>called</u> _____ her wedding just hours before the ceremony.

10. Never let Gustavo <u>borrow</u> money _____ you; you'll never
see it again!

11. <u>All</u> _____ <u>all</u>, it was a fabulous party!

12. Don't you <u>long</u> _____ the day that little robots will do all of
our household chores?

13. Even though I know that there is no <u>use</u> _____worrying,
I sometimes lie awake at night contemplating awful things that might
happen.

14. My teacher's explanations are long and unclear. I wish she'd just
<u>come</u> _____ the point!

15. My family usually eats at home, but _____ <u>occasion</u>, we
treat ourselves to a meal at a restaurant.

16. Because many parents don't <u>approve</u> _____ tattoos, teens
often don't tell them when they get one.

17. Anton is very <u>generous</u> _____ his car. He has allowed me
to borrow it several times when I desperately needed transportation.

18. The wind was blowing with such force that it nearly <u>knocked</u> me
_____ when I crossed the street.

19. Blue jeans <u>shrink</u> _____ hot water.

20. One of the <u>causes</u> _____ the American Civil War was slavery.

21. I just received an e-mail from Samantha. I can't wait to <u>reply</u>
_____ her.

DISCUSSION

1. When you are daydreaming about home, what three things do you most <u>long for</u>?

2. What are two <u>causes of</u> anger for you? How do you react when you get angry?

3. Name a celebrity with whom you think you have something <u>in common</u>. What interests/traits/values do you think that the two of you share?

4. Name an activity that you like to do only <u>on occasion</u>?

5. Do you <u>approve of</u> tattoos? Would you ever get one? Would you want you children to get one?

WEEK 7

MONDAY

1. Daniel didn't have a valid <u>reason</u> _____ being late to class today.

2. Elena was very <u>angry</u> _____ Alex when he forgot to pick her up for school.

3. It's good to let most things roll off your shoulders so that you only get <u>angry</u> _____ important matters.

4. Johnny's mother won't allow him to <u>associate</u> _____ anyone who's in a gang.

5. In what ways are you <u>similar</u> _____ your mother?

6. I've never been able to <u>turn</u> _____ dessert. Can you?

7. _____ <u>general</u>, I find my ESL class to be both challenging and interesting.

TUESDAY

1. Daniel didn't have a valid <u>reason</u> _____ being late to class today.

2. Elena was very <u>angry</u> _____ Alex when he forgot to pick her up for school.

3. It's good to let most things roll off your shoulders so that you only get <u>angry</u> _____ important matters.

4. Johnny's mother won't allow him to <u>associate</u> _____ anyone who's in a gang.

5. In what ways are you <u>similar</u> _____ your mother?

6. I've never been able to <u>turn</u> _____ dessert. Can you?

7. _____ <u>general</u>, I find my ESL class to be both challenging and interesting.

8. I'm so <u>fed</u> _____ _____ Stephan's bad temper. He jumps down my throat over every little mistake I make.

9. I've been absent from school for ten days. I don't know how I'll ever <u>catch up</u> _____ the class.

10. John was <u>overcome</u> _____ joy when his daughter got married.

11. Since yesterday's grammar was so difficult, Mrs. Chu decided to <u>go</u> _____ it again.

12. Kentaro called and said that he had something very important to <u>talk</u> _____ with me.

13. It's tragic that Peter has been <u>estranged</u> _____ his family for so many years. I wonder if they will ever reconcile.

14. Your name is George Washington! Are you <u>related</u> _____ the first president of the U.S.?

WEDNESDAY

1. Daniel didn't have a valid <u>reason</u> _____ being late to class today.

2. Elena was very <u>angry</u> _____ Alex when he forgot to pick her up for school.

3. It's good to let most things roll off your shoulders so that you only get <u>angry</u> _____ important matters.

4. Johnny's mother won't allow him to <u>associate</u> _____ anyone who's in a gang.

5. In what ways are you <u>similar</u> _____ your mother?

6. I've never been able to <u>turn</u> _____ dessert. Can you?

7. _____ general, I find my ESL class to be both challenging and interesting.

8. I'm so <u>fed</u> _____ _____ Stephan's bad temper. He jumps down my throat over every little mistake I make.

9. I've been absent from school for ten days. I don't know how I'll ever <u>catch up</u> _____the class.

10. John was <u>overcome</u> _____ joy when his daughter got married.

11. Since yesterday's grammar was so difficult, Mrs. Chu decided to <u>go</u> _____it again.

12. Kentaro called and said that he had something very important to <u>talk</u> _____ with me.

13. It's tragic that Peter has been <u>estranged</u> _____ his family for so many years. I wonder if they will ever reconcile.

14. Your name is George Washington! Are you <u>related</u> _____ the first president of the U.S.?

15. Classical music is very <u>pleasing</u> _____ my ear.

16. Nora is <u>interested</u> _____ taking a ballet class. Do you know where she can find one?

17. Tanya found an adorable kitten yesterday. It had no tags and she couldn't figure out whom it <u>belonged</u> _____.

18. Joan has an <u>affinity</u> _____ beaches and hot, sunny weather, while John loves mountains and snow. Can this marriage last?

19. If you want Ruth to be _____ <u>time</u> for an event, you have to tell her it begins an hour before it really starts!

20. People are beginning to <u>wonder</u> _____ the imminent effects of global warming on our planet.

21. I look like my father, but my personality is completely <u>different</u> _____ his.

THURSDAY

1. Daniel didn't have a valid <u>reason</u> _____ being late to class today.

2. Elena was very <u>angry</u> _____ Alex when he forgot to pick her up for school.

3. It's good to let most things roll off your shoulders so that you only get <u>angry</u> _____ important matters.

4. Johnny's mother won't allow him to <u>associate</u> _____ anyone who's in a gang.

5. In what ways are you <u>similar</u> _____ your mother?

6. I've never been able to <u>turn</u> _____ dessert. Can you?

7. _____ <u>general</u>, I find my ESL class to be both challenging and interesting.

8. I'm so <u>fed</u> _____ _____ Stephan's bad temper. He jumps down my throat over every little mistake I make.

9. I've been absent from school for ten days. I don't know how I'll ever <u>catch up</u> _____ the class.

10. John was <u>overcome</u> _____ joy when his daughter got married.

11. Since yesterday's grammar was so difficult, Mrs. Chu decided to <u>go</u> _____ it again.

12. Kentaro called and said that he had something very important to <u>talk</u> _____ with me.

13. It's tragic that Peter has been <u>estranged</u> _____ his family for so many years. I wonder if they will ever reconcile.

14. Your name is George Washington! Are you <u>related</u> _____ the first president of the U.S.?

15. Classical music is very <u>pleasing</u> _____ my ear.

16. Nora is <u>interested</u> _____ taking a ballet class. Do you know where she can find one?

17. Tanya found an adorable kitten yesterday. It had no tags and she couldn't figure out whom it <u>belonged</u> _____.

18. Joan has an <u>affinity</u> _____ beaches and hot, sunny weather, while John loves mountains and snow. Can this marriage last?

19. If you want Ruth to be _____ <u>time</u> for an event, you have to tell her it begins an hour before it really starts!

20. People are beginning to <u>wonder</u> _____ the imminent effects of global warming on our planet.

21. I look like my father, but my personality is completely <u>different</u> _____ his.

FRIDAY

1. Daniel didn't have a valid <u>reason</u> _____ being late to class today.

2. Elena was very <u>angry</u> _____ Alex when he forgot to pick her up for school.

3. It's good to let most things roll off your shoulders so that you only get <u>angry</u> _____ important matters.

4. Johnny's mother won't allow him to <u>associate</u> _____ anyone who's in a gang.

5. In what ways are you <u>similar</u> _____ your mother?

6. I've never been able to <u>turn</u> _____ dessert. Can you?

7. _____ <u>general</u>, I find my ESL class to be both challenging and interesting.

8. I'm so <u>fed</u> _____ _____ Stephan's bad temper. He jumps down my throat over every little mistake I make.

9. I've been absent from school for ten days. I don't know how I'll ever catch up _____ the class.

10. John was <u>overcome</u> _____ joy when his daughter got married.

11. Since yesterday's grammar was so difficult, Mrs. Chu decided to go _____ it again.

12. Kentaro called and said that he had something very important to <u>talk</u> _____ with me.

13. It's tragic that Peter has been <u>estranged</u> _____ his family for so many years. I wonder if they will ever reconcile.

14. Your name is George Washington! Are you <u>related</u> _____ the first president of the U.S.?

15. Classical music is very <u>pleasing</u> _____ my ear.

16. Nora is <u>interested</u> _____ taking a ballet class. Do you know where she can find one?

17. Tanya found an adorable kitten yesterday. It had no tags and she couldn't figure out whom it <u>belonged</u> _____.

18. Joan has an <u>affinity</u> _____ beaches and hot, sunny weather, while John loves mountains and snow. Can this marriage last?

19. If you want Ruth to be _____ <u>time</u> for an event, you have to tell her it begins an hour before it really starts!

20. People are beginning to <u>wonder</u> _____ the imminent effects of global warming on our planet.

21. I look like my father, but my personality is completely <u>different</u> _____ his.

DISCUSSION

1. What dessert do you never <u>turn down</u>?

2. Are you <u>related to</u> anyone famous? Who is he/she?

3. What kind of music is <u>pleasing to</u> you? What kind of music is <u>displeasing to</u> you?

4. Are you usually <u>on time</u> for appointments, or are you usually late?

5. In what ways are you <u>similar to</u> your mother? In what ways are you <u>different from</u> her?

WEEK 8

MONDAY

1. The doctor recommended that David should <u>cut down</u> _____ the amount of junk food that he eats.

2. Manuel travels so much for his business that I never know where he is _____ <u>one day to the next</u>.

3. I'm <u>looking</u> _____ Yale University. I hear that it has a great theater department.

4. Joanna was carried away by ambulance after she <u>passed</u> _____ _____ running in 100 degree heat.

5. Since he was a little boy, Toby has been <u>afraid</u> _____ dogs.

6. Did you hear that Miko's grandfather <u>passed</u> _____ last Friday?

7. I don't want to go to the amusement park. _____ <u>one thing</u>, I'm afraid of roller-coasters.

TUESDAY

1. The doctor recommended that David should <u>cut down</u> _____ the amount of junk food that he eats.

2. Manuel travels so much for his business that I never know where he is _____ <u>one day to the next</u>.

3. I'm <u>looking</u> _____ Yale University. I hear that it has a great theater department.

4. Joanna was carried away by ambulance after she <u>passed</u> _____ _____ running in 100 degree heat.

5. Since he was a little boy, Toby has been <u>afraid</u> _____ dogs.

6. Did you hear that Miko's grandfather <u>passed</u> _____ last Friday?

7. I don't want to go to the amusement park. _____ <u>one thing</u>, I'm afraid of roller-coasters.

8. _____ <u>another</u>, I hate crowds.

9. The new chancellor of the university wants to <u>bring</u> _____ real change in the admission policies.

10. Are you <u>certain</u> _____ your decision? Be sure. It might be difficult to change your mind later should you decide to.

11. No matter how much ice cream I eat, I never seem to get <u>enough</u> _____ it.

12. Sarah <u>argued</u> _____ her mother last night.

13. They <u>argued</u> _____ the hour that Sarah had to return from a party.

14. Tony sat <u>next</u> _____ Michael Jordan at the doctor's office yesterday. He asked him for an autograph.

WEDNESDAY

1. The doctor recommended that David should <u>cut down</u> _____ the amount of junk food that he eats.

2. Manuel travels so much for his business that I never know where he is _____ <u>one day to the next</u>.

3. I'm <u>looking</u> _____ Yale University. I hear that it has a great theater department.

4. Joanna was carried away by ambulance after she <u>passed</u> _____ _____ running in 100 degree heat.

5. Since he was a little boy, Toby has been <u>afraid</u> _____ dogs.

6. Did you hear that Miko's grandfather <u>passed</u> _____ last Friday?

7. I don't want to go to the amusement park. _____ <u>one thing</u>, I'm afraid of roller-coasters.

8. _____ another, I hate crowds.

9. The new chancellor of the university wants to <u>bring</u> _____ real change in the admission policies.

10. Are you <u>certain</u> _____ your decision? Be sure. It might be difficult to change your mind later should you decide to.

11. No matter how much ice cream I eat, I never seem to get <u>enough</u> _____ it.

12. Sarah <u>argued</u> _____ her mother last night.

13. They <u>argued</u> _____ the hour that Sarah had to return from a party.

14. Tony sat <u>next</u> _____ Michael Jordan at the doctor's office yesterday. He asked him for an autograph.

15. I don't think that I can <u>put up</u> _____ Timothy's bad mood today. I'm in a black mood myself!

16. Do you think that Michael Jordan was <u>superior</u> _____ every other basketball player in history?

17. How long has McDonald's been _____ <u>existence</u>? I think they've only been a chain since the 1960's.

18. What export is your country best <u>known</u> _____?

19. Tony applied for a job as an electrician, but I don't think that he's really <u>qualified</u> _____ it.

20. My aunt sent me $25 for my birthday. I think I'm going to <u>spend</u> it _____ a new blouse.

21. I was very <u>flattered</u> _____ my Biology teacher's praise for my experiment.

THURSDAY

1. The doctor recommended that David should <u>cut down</u> _____ the amount of junk food that he eats.

2. Manuel travels so much for his business that I never know where he is _____ one day to the next.

3. I'm looking _____ Yale University. I hear that it has a great theater department.

4. Joanna was carried away by ambulance after she passed _____ _____ running in 100 degree heat.

5. Since he was a little boy, Toby has been afraid _____ dogs.

6. Did you hear that Miko's grandfather passed _____ last Friday?

7. I don't want to go to the amusement park. _____ one thing, I'm afraid of roller-coasters.

8. _____ another, I hate crowds.

9. The new chancellor of the university wants to bring _____ real change in the admission policies.

10. Are you certain _____ your decision? Be sure. It might be difficult to change your mind later should you decide to.

11. No matter how much ice cream I eat, I never seem to get enough _____ it.

12. Sarah argued _____ her mother last night.

13. They argued _____ the hour that Sarah had to return from a party.

14. Tony sat next _____ Michael Jordan at the doctor's office yesterday. He asked him for an autograph.

15. I don't think that I can put up _____ Timothy's bad mood today. I'm in a black mood myself!

16. Do you think that Michael Jordan was superior _____ every other basketball player in history?

17. How long has McDonald's been _____ existence? I think they've only been a chain since the 1960's.

18. What export is your country best known _____?

19. Tony applied for a job as an electrician, but I don't think that he's really <u>qualified</u> _____ it.

20. My aunt sent me $25 for my birthday. I think I'm going to <u>spend</u> it _____ a new blouse.

21. I was very <u>flattered</u> _____ my Biology teacher's praise for my experiment.

FRIDAY

1. The doctor recommended that David should <u>cut down</u> _____ the amount of junk food that he eats.

2. Manuel travels so much for his business that I never know where he is _____ <u>one day to the next</u>.

3. I'm <u>looking</u> _____ Yale University. I hear that it has a great theater department.

4. Joanna was carried away by ambulance after she <u>passed</u> _____ _____ running in 100 degree heat.

5. Since he was a little boy, Toby has been <u>afraid</u> _____ dogs.

6. Did you hear that Miko's grandfather <u>passed</u> _____ last Friday?

7. I don't want to go to the amusement park. _____ <u>one thing</u>, I'm afraid of roller-coasters.

8. _____ <u>another</u>, I hate crowds.

9. The new chancellor of the university wants to <u>bring</u> _____ real change in the admission policies.

10. Are you <u>certain</u> _____ your decision? Be sure. It might be difficult to change your mind later should you decide to.

11. No matter how much ice cream I eat, I never seem to get <u>enough</u> _____ it.

12. Sarah <u>argued</u> _____ her mother last night.

13. They <u>argued</u> _____ the hour that Sarah had to return from a party.

14. Tony sat <u>next</u> _____ Michael Jordan at the doctor's office yesterday. He asked him for an autograph.

15. I don't think that I can <u>put up</u> _____ Timothy's bad mood today. I'm in a black mood myself!

16. Do you think that Michael Jordan was <u>superior</u> _____ every other basketball player in history?

17. How long has McDonald's been _____ <u>existence</u>? I think they've only been a chain since the 1960's.

18. What export is your country best <u>known</u> _____?

19. Tony applied for a job as an electrician, but I don't think that he's really <u>qualified</u> _____ it.

20. My aunt sent me $25 for my birthday. I think I'm going to <u>spend</u> it _____ a new blouse.

21. I was very <u>flattered</u> _____ my Biology teacher's praise for my experiment.

DISCUSSION

1. Are you <u>afraid of</u> anything? What is it? What do you do to diminish your fear?

2. What is your country best <u>known for</u>?

3. Congratulations! You have just found $25. What will you <u>spend</u> it <u>on</u>?

4. What personality traits do you have trouble <u>putting up with</u>?

5. What meal can you never get <u>enough of</u>?

REVIEW WEEKS 5-8

WEEK 5

1. Mr. Potter was always very <u>kind</u> _____ the children who lived in his neighborhood.

2. It was very <u>kind</u> _____ Mr. Potter to invite the children over to watch a movie at his house last Saturday.

3. Paula had to miss dance class yesterday <u>because</u> _____ her bad back.

4. The thieves <u>held</u> _____ the grocery store, stealing over $500.

5. _____ <u>retrospect</u>, I can't believe I turned Juan down when he asked me to marry him. What a mistake I made!

6. Many hours of studying <u>resulted</u> _____ my getting an "A" on the final examination.

7. An "A" on the final examination was <u>the result</u> _____ many hours of studying.

8. Toshiko always <u>smiles</u> _____ her customers.

9. I'm going to exercise in the park tomorrow <u>regardless</u> _____ the weather.

10. Would it be <u>possible</u> _____ you to give me a ride to class tomorrow night?

11. Let's <u>plan</u> _____ going to a movie this Saturday night.

12. Every <u>once</u> _____ <u>a while</u> it's fun to spend the entire after-noon gardening in my yard.

13. The picnic was canceled _____ <u>account</u> _____ bad weather.

14. When you were a teenager, did you always <u>listen</u> _____ your parents?

15. Mrs. Seeger is such a worry-wart! She <u>worries</u> _____ everything.

16. I don't want to <u>work</u> _____ Mayumi on the class project because she never completes her work on time.

17. The English teacher can't <u>account</u> _____ five of her class grammar books. Where could they have gone?

18. It's very difficult to get <u>accustomed</u> _____ the customs of a new country.

19. <u>As a result</u> _____ yesterday's election, Tony is the new president of the school.

20. Mrs. Garcia is <u>resigned</u> _____ studying day and night this year for her TOEFL exam. She knows that she must do well on it, so she has made up her mind to give it her best shot.

21. Let's <u>take a chance</u> _____ the new pizzeria that just opened. Okay?

WEEK 6

1. Jonas was <u>doubtful</u> _____ his decision to fly east to attend his cousin's wedding. The flight was just too expensive.

2. _____ <u>times</u> I dream of dropping everything and moving to Tahiti.

3. Benjamin and I went out on our first date last night, but we had nothing _____ <u>common</u>.

4. How old were you when you stopped <u>believing</u> _____ Santa Claus?

5. The tag says that this sleeping bag is <u>suitable</u> _____ weather conditions as cold as 0 degrees centigrade.

6. Paul quickly <u>succumbed</u> _____ Peggy's quirky, funny personality and fell head over heels in love with her.

7. _____ the <u>time being</u>, John is working as a substitute teacher. He hopes that a full-time job will become available soon.

8. <u>First</u> _____ <u>all</u>, never cross the street without looking in both directions.

9. Tina <u>called</u> _____ her wedding just hours before the ceremony.

10. Never let Gustavo <u>borrow</u> money _____ you; you'll never see it again!

11. <u>All</u> _____ <u>all</u>, it was a fabulous party!

12. Don't you <u>long</u> _____ the day that little robots will do all of our household chores?

13. Even though I know that there is no <u>use</u> _____worrying, I sometimes lie awake at night contemplating awful things that might happen.

14. My teacher's explanations are long and unclear. I wish she'd just <u>come</u> _____ the point!

15. My family usually eats at home, but _____ <u>occasion</u>, we treat ourselves to a meal at a restaurant.

16. Because many parents don't <u>approve</u> _____ tattoos, teens often don't tell them when they get one.

17. Anton is very <u>generous</u> _____ his car. He has allowed me to borrow it several times when I desperately needed transportation.

18. The wind was blowing with such force that it nearly <u>knocked</u> me _____ when I crossed the street.

19. Blue jeans <u>shrink</u> _____ hot water.

20. One of the <u>causes</u> _____ the American Civil War was slavery.

21. I just received an e-mail from Samantha. I can't wait to <u>reply</u> _____ her.

WEEK 7

1. Daniel didn't have a valid <u>reason</u> _____ being late to class today.

2. Elena was very <u>angry</u> _____ Alex when he forgot to pick her up for school.

3. It's good to let most things roll off your shoulders so that you only get <u>angry</u> _____ important matters.

4. Johnny's mother won't allow him to <u>associate</u> _____ anyone who's in a gang.

5. In what ways are you <u>similar</u> _____ your mother?

6. I've never been able to <u>turn</u> _____ dessert. Can you?

7. _____ <u>general</u>, I find my ESL class to be both challenging and interesting.

8. I'm so <u>fed</u> _____ _____ Stephan's bad temper. He jumps down my throat over every little mistake I make.

9. I've been absent from school for ten days. I don't know how I'll ever <u>catch up</u> _____ the class.

10. John was <u>overcome</u> _____ joy when his daughter got married.

11. Since yesterday's grammar was so difficult, Mrs. Chu decided to <u>go</u> _____ it again.

12. Kentaro called and said that he had something very important to <u>talk</u> _____ with me.

13. It's tragic that Peter has been <u>estranged</u> _____ his family for so many years. I wonder if they will ever reconcile.

14. Your name is George Washington! Are you <u>related</u> _____ the first president of the U.S.?

15. Classical music is very <u>pleasing</u> _____ my ear.

16. Nora is <u>interested</u> _____ taking a ballet class. Do you know where she can find one?

17. Tanya found an adorable kitten yesterday. It had no tags and she couldn't figure out whom it <u>belonged</u> _____.

18. Joan has an <u>affinity</u> _____ beaches and hot, sunny weather, while John loves mountains and snow. Can this marriage last?

19. If you want Ruth to be _____ <u>time</u> for an event, you have to tell her it begins an hour before it really starts!

20. People are beginning to <u>wonder</u> _____ the imminent effects of global warming on our planet.

21. I look like my father, but my personality is completely <u>different</u> _____ his.

WEEK 8

1. The doctor recommended that David should <u>cut down</u> _____ the amount of junk food that he eats.

2. Manuel travels so much for his business that I never know where he is _____ <u>one day to the next</u>.

3. I'm <u>looking</u> _____ Yale University. I hear that it has a great theater department.

4. Joanna was carried away by ambulance after she <u>passed</u> _____ _____ running in 100 degree heat.

5. Since he was a little boy, Toby has been <u>afraid</u> _____ dogs.

6. Did you hear that Miko's grandfather <u>passed</u> _____ last Friday?

7. I don't want to go to the amusement park. _____ <u>one thing</u>, I'm afraid of roller-coasters.

8. _____ <u>another</u>, I hate crowds.

9. The new chancellor of the university wants to <u>bring</u> _____real change in the admission policies.

10. Are you <u>certain</u> _____ your decision? Be sure. It might be difficult to change your mind later should you decide to.

11. No matter how much ice cream I eat, I never seem to get <u>enough</u> _____ it.

12. Sarah <u>argued</u> _____ her mother last night.

13. They <u>argued</u> _____ the hour that Sarah had to return from a party.

14. Tony sat <u>next</u> _____ Michael Jordan at the doctor's office yesterday. He asked him for an autograph.

15. I don't think that I can <u>put up</u> _____ Timothy's bad mood today. I'm in a black mood myself!

16. Do you think that Michael Jordan was <u>superior</u> _____ every other basketball player in history?

17. How long has McDonald's been _____ <u>existence</u>? I think they've only been a chain since the 1960's.

18. What export is your country best <u>known</u> _____?

19. Tony applied for a job as an electrician, but I don't think that he's really <u>qualified</u> _____ it.

20. My aunt sent me $25 for my birthday. I think I'm going to <u>spend</u> it _____ a new blouse.

21. I was very <u>flattered</u> _____ my Biology teacher's praise for my experiment.

WEEK 9

MONDAY

1. I need to <u>look</u> _____ my notes one last time before the exam tomorrow.

2. The American public is increasingly <u>skeptical</u> _____ its politicians.

3. Because Juan was always <u>curious</u> _____ life in the future, when he became terminally ill, he paid to have his body frozen at death so that he could eventually be brought back to life.

4. Benjamin Franklin is very <u>famous</u> _____ his scientific experiments with electricity.

5. Maria is having trouble <u>deciding</u> _____ which dress she should wear to the prom.

6. Mr. Martinelli remembers that his teachers were <u>prejudiced</u> _____ minorities when he was in school in the 1940's.

7. I used to smoke two packs of cigarettes a day, but that was _____ <u>the past</u>.

TUESDAY

1. I need to <u>look</u> _____ my notes one last time before the exam tomorrow.

2. The American public is increasingly <u>skeptical</u> _____ its politicians.

3. Because Juan was always <u>curious</u> _____ life in the future, when he became terminally ill, he paid to have his body frozen at death so that he could eventually be brought back to life.

4. Benjamin Franklin is very <u>famous</u> _____ his scientific experiments with electricity.

5. Maria is having trouble <u>deciding</u> _____ which dress she should wear to the prom.

6. Mr. Martinelli remembers that his teachers were <u>prejudiced</u> _____ minorities when he was in school in the 1940's.

7. I used to smoke two packs of cigarettes a day, but that was _____ <u>the past</u>.

8. Because Norman is <u>intent</u> _____ getting a promotion, he puts in a lot of overtime.

9. American school children have to learn the Pledge of Allegiance _____ <u>heart</u> when they are in 1st grade.

10. Marcy<u> wastes</u> so much money _____ manicures and pedicures. Don't you think she'd be better using that money to pay off her credit cards?

11. I've never traveled outside of the USA. In fact, my travel experience has been <u>confined</u> _____ southern California.

12. Sylvia's hairstyle is hopelessly <u>out</u> _____ <u>date</u>. She's worn that style since 1951.

13. It's going to take five trips to <u>carry</u> _____ all of the trash from last night's party.

14. Teri deserves to "Ace" her math class <u>after</u> <u>all</u> _____ the time she's spent studying.

WEDNESDAY

1. I need to <u>look</u> _____ my notes one last time before the exam tomorrow.

2. The American public is increasingly <u>skeptical</u> _____ its politicians.

3. Because Juan was always <u>curious</u> _____ life in the future, when he became terminally ill, he paid to have his body frozen at death so that he could eventually be brought back to life.

4. Benjamin Franklin is very <u>famous</u> _____ his scientific experiments with electricity.

5. Maria is having trouble <u>deciding</u> _____ which dress she should wear to the prom.

6. Mr. Martinelli remembers that his teachers were <u>prejudiced</u> _____ minorities when he was in school in the 1940's.

7. I used to smoke two packs of cigarettes a day, but that was _____ <u>the past</u>.

8. Because Norman is <u>intent</u> _____ getting a promotion, he puts in a lot of overtime.

9. American school children have to learn the Pledge of Allegiance _____ <u>heart</u> when they are in 1st grade.

10. Marcy <u>wastes</u> so much money _____ manicures and pedicures. Don't you think she'd be better using that money to pay off her credit cards?

11. I've never traveled outside of the USA. In fact, my travel experience has been <u>confined</u> _____ southern California.

12. Sylvia's hairstyle is hopelessly <u>out</u> _____ <u>date</u>. She's worn that style since 1951.

13. It's going to take five trips to <u>carry</u> _____ all of the trash from last night's party.

14. Teri deserves to "Ace" her math class <u>after</u> <u>all</u> _____ the time she's spent studying.

15. As Luis sat on the jury, he became more and more <u>convinced</u> _____ the accused's innocence.

16. There can be a <u>maximum</u> _____ only twenty people in this elevator.

17. To be <u>eligible</u> _____ this job, the applicant must have at least five years experience.

18. The picnic is planned for Sunday, so let's <u>hope</u> _____ warm weather.

19. It's impossible to spend time with Stanley. All he does is <u>boast</u> _____ his son's accomplishments.

20. Don't <u>boast</u> _____ your colleagues about your job promotion. It'll make them feel jealous.

21. I've been <u>wrestling</u> _____ a dilemma: should I quit my job at the store to pursue my singing career or is that just foolish?

THURSDAY

1. I need to <u>look</u> _____ my notes one last time before the exam tomorrow.

2. The American public is increasingly <u>skeptical</u> _____ its politicians.

3. Because Juan was always <u>curious</u> _____ life in the future, when he became terminally ill, he paid to have his body frozen at death so that he could eventually be brought back to life.

4. Benjamin Franklin is very <u>famous</u> _____ his scientific experiments with electricity.

5. Maria is having trouble <u>deciding</u> _____ which dress she should wear to the prom.

6. Mr. Martinelli remembers that his teachers were <u>prejudiced</u> _____ minorities when he was in school in the 1940's.

7. I used to smoke two packs of cigarettes a day, but that was _____ the past.

8. Because Norman is intent _____ getting a promotion, he puts in a lot of overtime.

9. American school children have to learn the Pledge of Allegiance _____ heart when they are in 1ˢᵗ grade.

10. Marcy wastes so much money _____ manicures and pedicures. Don't you think she'd be better using that money to pay off her credit cards?

11. I've never traveled outside of the USA. In fact, my travel experience has been confined _____ southern California.

12. Sylvia's hairstyle is hopelessly out _____ date. She's worn that style since 1951.

13. It's going to take five trips to carry _____ all of the trash from last night's party.

14. Teri deserves to "Ace" her math class after all _____ the time she's spent studying.

15. As Luis sat on the jury, he became more and more convinced _____ the accused's innocence.

16. There can be a maximum _____ only twenty people in this elevator.

17. To be eligible _____ this job, the applicant must have at least five years experience.

18. The picnic is planned for Sunday, so let's hope _____ warm weather.

19. It's impossible to spend time with Stanley. All he does is boast _____ his son's accomplishments.

20. Don't boast _____ your colleagues about your job promotion. It'll make them feel jealous.

21. I've been <u>wrestling</u> _____ a dilemma: should I quit my job at the store to pursue my singing career or is that just foolish?

FRIDAY

1. I need to <u>look</u> _____ my notes one last time before the exam tomorrow.

2. The American public is increasingly <u>skeptical</u> _____ its politicians.

3. Because Juan was always <u>curious</u> _____ life in the future, when he became terminally ill, he paid to have his body frozen at death so that he could eventually be brought back to life.

4. Benjamin Franklin is very <u>famous</u> _____ his scientific experiments with electricity.

5. Maria is having trouble <u>deciding</u> _____ which dress she should wear to the prom.

6. Mr. Martinelli remembers that his teachers were <u>prejudiced</u> _____ minorities when he was in school in the 1940's.

7. I used to smoke two packs of cigarettes a day, but that was _____ <u>the past</u>.

8. Because Norman is <u>intent</u> _____ getting a promotion, he puts in a lot of overtime.

9. American school children have to learn the Pledge of Allegiance _____ <u>heart</u> when they are in 1st grade.

10. Marcy <u>wastes</u> so much money _____ manicures and pedicures. Don't you think she'd be better using that money to pay off her credit cards?

11. I've never traveled outside of the USA. In fact, my travel experience has been <u>confined</u> _____ southern California.

12. Sylvia's hairstyle is hopelessly <u>out</u> ____ _____ <u>date</u>. She's worn that style since 1951.

13. It's going to take five trips to <u>carry</u> _____ all of the trash from last night's party.

14. Teri deserves to "Ace" her math class <u>after all</u> _____ the time she's spent studying.

15. As Luis sat on the jury, he became more and more <u>convinced</u> _____ the accused's innocence.

16. There can be a <u>maximum</u> _____ only twenty people in this elevator.

17. To be <u>eligible</u> _____ this job, the applicant must have at least five years experience.

18. The picnic is planned for Sunday, so let's <u>hope</u> _____ warm weather.

19. It's impossible to spend time with Stanley. All he does is <u>boast</u> _____ his son's accomplishments.

20. Don't <u>boast</u> _____ your colleagues about your job promotion. It'll make them feel jealous.

21. I've been <u>wrestling</u> _____ a dilemma: should I quit my job at the store to pursue my singing career or is that just foolish?

DISCUSSION

1. Do you know you country's national anthem <u>by heart</u>? Sing the beginning of it to your partner.

2. What do you most enjoy <u>wasting</u> money <u>on</u>?

3. Name three things you <u>hope for</u> in the future.

4. Name a famous person from you country. What is he/she <u>famous for</u>?

5. Name two things that you are <u>intent upon</u> accomplishing this year.

WEEK 10

MONDAY

1. Cindy was <u>ashamed</u> _____ the loud voice that her father used when he was in public.

2. John always <u>shows</u> _____ late to office meetings. The boss is starting to get annoyed.

3. If Roget wants to <u>succeed</u> _____ the piano, he's going to have to practice a lot more than he does presently.

4. Have you ever seen the film "The Shawshank Redemption"? It's the story of one man's <u>escape</u> _____ prison.

5. I wish they would <u>turn</u> _____ the heat in the theater. I'm freezing!

6. Children are usually taught to <u>beware</u> _____ strangers. This advice is especially good in today's dangerous world.

7. As Shelly became more and more depressed, she increasingly <u>withdrew</u> _____ social activities and friends.

TUESDAY

1. Cindy was <u>ashamed</u> _____ the loud voice that her father used when he was in public.

2. John always <u>shows</u> _____ late to office meetings. The boss is starting to get annoyed.

3. If Roget wants to <u>succeed</u> _____ the piano, he's going to have to practice a lot more than he does presently.

4. Have you ever seen the film "The Shawshank Redemption"? It's the story of one man's <u>escape</u> _____ prison.

5. I wish they would <u>turn</u> _____ the heat in the theater. I'm freezing!

6. Children are usually taught to <u>beware</u> _____ strangers. This advice is especially good in today's dangerous world.

7. As Shelly became more and more depressed, she increasingly <u>withdrew</u> _____ social activities and friends.

8. How many days have you been <u>absent</u> _____ class? It seems as though you've been gone forever!

9. Timothy is so <u>careless</u> _____ what he says in front of other people. Just yesterday, he told everyone my deepest secret!

10. _____ <u>long</u>, you will have finished your program and will be a dental hygienist. Congratulations!

11. Look at the necklace. It's completely <u>composed</u> _____ sea shells.

12. Mrs. Stasick is the meanest teacher I've ever had. She <u>sneers</u> _____ all of the students, making us feel inferior and stupid. I don't understand why she continues to teach.

13 Can you believe that Annalie's wedding gown was completely sewn _____ <u>hand</u>?

14. I <u>gave</u> _____ temptation and ate an entire box of choco-late. Yum!

WEDNESDAY

1. Cindy was <u>ashamed</u> _____ the loud voice that her father used when he was in public.

2. John always <u>shows</u> _____ late to office meetings. The boss is starting to get annoyed.

3. If Roget wants to <u>succeed</u> _____ the piano, he's going to have to practice a lot more than he does presently.

4. Have you ever seen the film "The Shawshank Redemption"? It's the story of one man's <u>escape</u> _____ prison.

5. I wish they would <u>turn</u> _____ the heat in the theater. I'm freezing!

6. Children are usually taught to <u>beware</u> _____ strangers. This advice is especially good in today's dangerous world.

7. As Shelly became more and more depressed, she increasingly <u>withdrew</u> _____ social activities and friends.

8. How many days have you been <u>absent</u> _____ class? It seems as though you've been gone forever!

9. Timothy is so <u>careless</u> _____ what he says in front of other people. Just yesterday, he told everyone my deepest secret!

10. _____ <u>long</u>, you will have finished your program and will be a dental hygienist. Congratulations!

11. Look at the necklace. It's completely <u>composed</u> _____ sea shells.

12. Mrs. Stasick is the meanest teacher I've ever had. She <u>sneers</u> _____ all of the students, making us feel inferior and stupid. I don't understand why she continues to teach.

13. Can you believe that Annalie's wedding gown was completely sewn _____ <u>hand</u>?

14. I <u>gave</u> _____ temptation and ate an entire box of chocolate. Yum!

15. For me, the beach is always <u>preferable</u> _____ the mountains. How about for you?

16. Stephen is so <u>enthusiastic</u> _____ the Yankees that he knows every possible statistic about the team and its players.

17. Because of the construction, they had to <u>detour</u> _____ the main highway.

18. Val's always been <u>jealous</u> _____ Susan's jet black hair, while Susan has always hated it.

19. It looked as though that car smacked into the mailbox _____ <u>purpose</u>.

20. <u>All</u> _____ <u>a sudden</u> the beautiful sky was replaced by a dark, threatening one.

21. _____ <u>the most part</u>, this has been the most wonderful vacation of my life.

THURSDAY

1. Cindy was <u>ashamed</u> _____ the loud voice that her father used when he was in public.

2. John always <u>shows</u> _____ late to office meetings. The boss is starting to get annoyed.

3. If Roget wants to <u>succeed</u> _____ the piano, he's going to have to practice a lot more than he does presently.

4. Have you ever seen the film "The Shawshank Redemption"? It's the story of one man's <u>escape</u> _____ prison.

5. I wish they would <u>turn</u> _____ the heat in the theater. I'm freezing!

6. Children are usually taught to <u>beware</u> _____ strangers. This advice is especially good in today's dangerous world.

7. As Shelly became more and more depressed, she increasingly <u>withdrew</u> _____ social activities and friends.

8. How many days have you been <u>absent</u> _____ class? It seems as though you've been gone forever!

9. Timothy is so <u>careless</u> _____ what he says in front of other people. Just yesterday, he told everyone my deepest secret!

10. _____ long, you will have finished your program and will be a dental hygienist. Congratulations!

11. Look at the necklace. It's completely composed _____ sea shells.

12. Mrs. Stasick is the meanest teacher I've ever had. She sneers _____ all of the students, making us feel inferior and stupid. I don't understand why she continues to teach.

13. Can you believe that Annalie's wedding gown was completely sewn _____ hand?

14. I gave _____ temptation and ate an entire box of chocolate. Yum!

15. For me, the beach is always preferable _____ the mountains. How about for you?

16. Stephen is so enthusiastic _____ the Yankees that he knows every possible statistic about the team and its players.

17. Because of the construction, they had to detour _____ the main highway.

18. Val's always been jealous _____ Susan's jet black hair, while Susan has always hated it.

19. It looked as though that car smacked into the mailbox _____ purpose.

20. All _____ a sudden the beautiful sky was replaced by a dark, threatening one.

21. _____ the most part, this has been the most wonderful vacation of my life.

FRIDAY

1. Cindy was ashamed _____ the loud voice that her father used when he was in public.

2. John always <u>shows</u> _____ late to office meetings. The boss is starting to get annoyed.

3. If Roget wants to <u>succeed</u> _____ the piano, he's going to have to practice a lot more than he does presently.

4. Have you ever seen the film "The Shawshank Redemption"? It's the story of one man's <u>escape</u> _____ prison.

5. I wish they would <u>turn</u> _____ the heat in the theater. I'm freezing!

6. Children are usually taught to <u>beware</u> _____ strangers. This advice is especially good in today's dangerous world.

7. As Shelly became more and more depressed, she increasingly <u>withdrew</u> _____ social activities and friends.

8. How many days have you been <u>absent</u> _____ class? It seems as though you've been gone forever!

9. Timothy is so <u>careless</u> _____ what he says in front of other people. Just yesterday, he told everyone my deepest secret!

10. _____ <u>long</u>, you will have finished your program and will be a dental hygienist. Congratulations!

11. Look at the necklace. It's completely <u>composed</u> _____ sea shells.

12. Mrs. Stasick is the meanest teacher I've ever had. She <u>sneers</u> _____ all of the students, making us feel inferior and stupid. I don't understand why she continues to teach.

13. Can you believe that Annalie's wedding gown was completely sewn _____ <u>hand</u>?

14. I <u>gave</u> _____ temptation and ate an entire box of choco-late. Yum!

15. For me, the beach is always <u>preferable</u> _____ the mountains. How about for you?

16. Stephen is so <u>enthusiastic</u> _____ the Yankees that he knows every possible statistic about the team and its players.

17. Because of the construction, they had to <u>detour</u> _____ the main highway.

18. Val's always been <u>jealous</u> _____ Susan's jet black hair, while Susan has always hated it.

19. It looked as though that car smacked into the mailbox _____ <u>purpose</u>.

20. <u>All</u> _____ <u>a sudden</u> the beautiful sky was replaced by a dark, threatening one.

21. _____ <u>the most part</u>, this has been the most wonderful vacation of my life.

DISCUSSION

1. What activities are you very <u>enthusiastic about</u>?

2. <u>For the most part</u>, how do you like to spend your free time?

3. If you have only one vacation a year, which would be <u>preferable to</u> you - the beach or the mountains?

4. When you <u>give into</u> temptation, what do you eat/drink/do?

5. How many nationalities is our class <u>composed of</u> today? (Take a guess and then we'll determine the actual number.)

WEEK 11

MONDAY

1. Why is Miguel always _____ such <u>a hurry</u>?

2. Unfortunately, we <u>based</u> our decision _____ information that proved to be untrue.

3. Many people believe that society should <u>do away</u> _____ the death penalty.

4. That professor is so boring. Her lectures <u>go</u> _____ and _____.

5. I hope that Mr. Rafferty doesn't <u>call</u> _____ me today because I didn't have time to complete my homework.

6. I don't <u>feel</u> <u>sorry</u> _____ for Alex. I know he lost his job, but he was fired because he was lazy and had a terrible attitude.

7. Eve explained how <u>sorry</u> she was _____ missing the party last night, but she had to work late into the night.

TUESDAY

1. Why is Miguel always _____ such <u>a hurry</u>?

2. Unfortunately, we <u>based</u> our decision _____ information that proved to be untrue.

3. Many people believe that society should <u>do away</u> _____ the death penalty.

4. That professor is so boring. Her lectures <u>go</u> _____ and _____.

5. I hope that Mr. Rafferty doesn't <u>call</u> _____ me today because I didn't have time to complete my homework.

6. I don't <u>feel</u> <u>sorry</u> _____ for Alex. I know he lost his job, but he was fired because he was lazy and had a terrible attitude.

7. Eve explained how <u>sorry</u> she was _____ missing the party last night, but she had to work late into the night.

8. Let's go out for dinner <u>instead</u> _____ eating at home tonight.

9. It's time for the Smiths to <u>get rid</u> _____ their old jalopy, don't you think? It's not dependable anymore.

10. It was <u>considerate</u> _____ Pablo to invite Teresa to his birthday party since she's new in town and knows very few people.

11. <u>Watch out</u> _____ jelly fish at the beach in August. Their sting really hurts.

12. I'll meet you on the corner of Main and Maple at 5:00. <u>Watch</u> _____ me.

13. The child seat law may be inconvenient, but it was <u>passed</u> _____ the safety of children.

14. Emily and Eric <u>agree</u> _____ absolutely nothing. How do they stay married?

WEDNESDAY

1. Why is Miguel always _____ such <u>a hurry</u>?

2. Unfortunately, we <u>based</u> our decision _____ information that proved to be untrue.

3. Many people believe that society should <u>do away</u> _____ the death penalty.

4. That professor is so boring. Her lectures <u>go</u> _____ and _____.

5. I hope that Mr. Rafferty doesn't <u>call</u> _____ me today because I didn't have time to complete my homework.

6. I don't <u>feel</u> <u>sorry</u> _____ for Alex. I know he lost his job, but he was fired because he was lazy and had a terrible attitude.

7. Eve explained how <u>sorry</u> she was _____ missing the party last night, but she had to work late into the night.

8. Let's go out for dinner <u>instead</u> _____ eating at home tonight.

9. It's time for the Smiths to <u>get rid</u> _____ their old jalopy, don't you think? It's not dependable anymore.

10. It was <u>considerate</u> _____ Pablo to invite Teresa to his birthday party since she's new in town and knows very few people.

11. <u>Watch out</u> _____ jelly fish at the beach in August. Their sting really hurts.

12. I'll meet you on the corner of Main and Maple at 5:00. <u>Watch</u> _____ me.

13. The child seat law may be inconvenient, but it was <u>passed</u> _____ the safety of children.

14. Emily and Eric <u>agree</u> _____ absolutely nothing. How do they stay married?

15. Judy and Mike don't <u>agree</u> _____ each other about politics – she's a Democrat and he's a Republican.

16. I've been <u>hooked</u> _____ reading for as long as I can remember.

17. Why did the city <u>tear</u> _____ the Cove Theater? I loved that old building!

18. Whenever I'm sad, I <u>cheer</u> <u>myself</u> _____ by sitting on my couch with a great big bowl of gooey chocolate ice cream and a spoon. Then, I happily watch one of my favorite old movies.

19. It's <u>evident</u> _____ Ali's behavior that he isn't interested in Mariline anymore.

20. Don't forget to <u>turn</u> _____ your essay tomorrow. If it's late, you'll have an entire letter grade deducted.

21. A great job <u>combines</u> interesting work _____ good pay and good working conditions.

THURSDAY

1. Why is Miguel always _____ such <u>a hurry</u>?

2. Unfortunately, we <u>based</u> our decision _____ information that proved to be untrue.

3. Many people believe that society should <u>do away</u> _____ the death penalty.

4. That professor is so boring. Her lectures <u>go</u> _____ and _____.

5. I hope that Mr. Rafferty doesn't <u>call</u> _____ me today because I didn't have time to complete my homework.

6. I don't <u>feel</u> <u>sorry</u> _____ for Alex. I know he lost his job, but he was fired because he was lazy and had a terrible attitude.

7. Eve explained how <u>sorry</u> she was _____ missing the party last night, but she had to work late into the night.

8. Let's go out for dinner <u>instead</u> _____ eating at home tonight.

9. It's time for the Smiths to <u>get rid</u> _____ their old jalopy, don't you think? It's not dependable anymore.

10. It was <u>considerate</u> _____ Pablo to invite Teresa to his birthday party since she's new in town and knows very few people.

11. <u>Watch out</u> _____ jelly fish at the beach in August. Their sting really hurts.

12. I'll meet you on the corner of Main and Maple at 5:00. <u>Watch</u> _____ me.

13. The child seat law may be inconvenient, but it was <u>passed</u> _____ the safety of children.

14. Emily and Eric <u>agree</u> _____ absolutely nothing. How do they stay married?

15. Judy and Mike don't <u>agree</u> _____ each other about politics – she's a Democrat and he's a Republican.

16. I've been <u>hooked</u> _____ reading for as long as I can remember.

17. Why did the city <u>tear</u> _____ the Cove Theater? I loved that old building!

18. Whenever I'm sad, I <u>cheer</u> <u>myself</u> _____ by sitting on my couch with a great big bowl of gooey chocolate ice cream and a spoon. Then, I happily watch one of my favorite old movies.

19. It's <u>evident</u> _____ Ali''s behavior that he isn't interested in Mariline anymore.

20. Don't forget to <u>turn</u> _____ your essay tomorrow. If it's late, you'll have an entire letter grade deducted.

21. A great job <u>combines</u> interesting work _____ good pay and good working conditions.

FRIDAY

1. Why is Miguel always _____ such <u>a hurry</u>?

2. Unfortunately, we <u>based</u> our decision _____ information that proved to be untrue.

3. Many people believe that society should <u>do away</u> _____ the death penalty.

4. That professor is so boring. Her lectures <u>go</u> _____ and _____ .

5. I hope that Mr. Rafferty doesn't <u>call</u> _____ me today because I didn't have time to complete my homework.

6. I don't <u>feel</u> <u>sorry</u> _____ for Alex. I know he lost his job, but he was fired because he was lazy and had a terrible attitude.

7. Eve explained how <u>sorry</u> she was _____ missing the party last night, but she had to work late into the night.

8. Let's go out for dinner <u>instead</u> _____ eating at home tonight.

9. It's time for the Smiths to <u>get rid</u> _____ their old jalopy, don't you think? It's not dependable anymore.

10. It was <u>considerate</u> _____ Pablo to invite Teresa to his birthday party since she's new in town and knows very few people.

11. <u>Watch out</u> _____ jelly fish at the beach in August. Their sting really hurts.

12. I'll meet you on the corner of Main and Maple at 5:00. <u>Watch</u> _____ me.

13. The child seat law may be inconvenient, but it was <u>passed</u> _____ the safety of children.

14. Emily and Eric <u>agree</u> _____ absolutely nothing. How do they stay married?

15. Judy and Mike don't <u>agree</u> _____ each other about politics – she's a Democrat and he's a Republican.

16. I've been <u>hooked</u> _____ reading for as long as I can remember.

17. Why did the city <u>tear</u> _____ the Cove Theater? I loved that old building!

18. Whenever I'm sad, I <u>cheer</u> <u>myself</u> _____ by sitting on my couch with a great big bowl of gooey chocolate ice cream and a spoon. Then, I happily watch one of my favorite old movies.

19. It's <u>evident</u> _____ Ali's behavior that he isn't interested in Mariline anymore.

20. Don't forget to <u>turn</u> _____ your essay tomorrow. If it's late, you'll have an entire letter grade deducted.

21. A great job <u>combines</u> interesting work _____ good pay and good working conditions.

DISCUSSION

1. Do you believe that society should <u>do away with </u>the death penalty? Why or why not?

2. If you could be doing anything at all right now <u>instead of</u> sitting in English class, what would you be doing? Where would you be doing it?

3. What do you do to <u>cheer</u> <u>yourself</u> <u>up</u> when you are sad? If you were to watch a movie, which movie would you watch?

4. Are you generally relaxed in the mornings or are you <u>in a hurry</u>? How can you simplify you morning routine?

5. Would you <u>agree with</u> someone to gain 50 pounds if you were to be paid $10,000 for doing so? How much money would you take to gain 50 pounds?

WEEK 12

MONDAY

1.   After Lettie betrayed me by revealing my secret to her friends, I <u>crossed</u> her _____ my list of friends.

2. It was <u>good</u> _____ Daniel to drive his grandmother to her bridge game.

3. I'm _____ my <u>worst</u> in the morning before my first cup of coffee.

4. I'm _____ my <u>best</u> after I've had a day off from work and have had a chance to take a long, luxurious nap.

5. Lorena <u>complained</u> _____ her supervisor about a co-worker's racial slurs.

6. The fans in the stadium <u>jeered</u> _____ the tennis player after he showed poor sportsmanship.

7. _____ <u>all means</u>, bring your new girlfriend to the party on Saturday. I can't wait to meet her!

TUESDAY

1.   After Lettie betrayed me by revealing my secret to her friends, I <u>crossed</u> her _____ my list of friends.

2. It was <u>good</u> _____ Daniel to drive his grandmother to her bridge game.

3. I'm _____ my <u>worst</u> in the morning before my first cup of coffee.

4. I'm _____ my <u>best</u> after I've had a day off from work and have had a chance to take a long, luxurious nap.

5. Lorena <u>complained</u> _____ her supervisor about a co-worker's racial slurs.

6. The fans in the stadium <u>jeered</u> _____ the tennis player after he showed poor sportsmanship.

7. _____ <u>all means</u>, bring your new girlfriend to the party on Saturday. I can't wait to meet her!

8. Are you _____ <u>favor</u> _____ the new tax cut proposals, or are you opposed to them?

9. Jan has no real job. She just lives <u>day</u> _____ <u>day.</u>

10. _____ <u>time</u> _____ <u>time</u>, I really enjoy an ice cream sundae dripping with hot fudge and whipped cream.

11. My essay was so full of grammatical errors that my teacher is making me <u>do</u> it _____.

12. I bought the wrong book _____ <u>mistake</u>. Now I have to return it to the bookstore.

13. I don't mind _____ <u>the least</u> if Patty and her fiancé come for dinner on Friday night.

14. What holiday do you most <u>look forward</u> _____? For me, it's Thanksgiving.

WEDNESDAY

1. After Lettie betrayed me by revealing my secret to her friends, I <u>crossed</u> her _____ my list of friends.

2. It was <u>good</u> _____ Daniel to drive his grandmother to her bridge game.

3. I'm _____ my <u>worst</u> in the morning before my first cup of coffee.

4. I'm _____ my <u>best</u> after I've had a day off from work and have had a chance to take a long, luxurious nap.

5. Lorena complained _____ her supervisor about a co-worker's racial slurs.

6. The fans in the stadium jeered _____ the tennis player after he showed poor sportsmanship.

7. _____ all means, bring your new girlfriend to the party on Saturday. I can't wait to meet her!

8. Are you _____ favor _____ the new tax cut proposals, or are you opposed to them?

9. Jan has no real job. She just lives day _____ day.

10. _____ time _____ time, I really enjoy an ice cream sundae dripping with hot fudge and whipped cream.

11. My essay was so full of grammatical errors that my teacher is making me do it _____.

12. I bought the wrong book _____ mistake. Now I have to return it to the bookstore.

13. I don't mind _____ the least if Patty and her fiancé come for dinner on Friday night.

14. What holiday do you most look forward _____? For me, it's Thanksgiving.

15. Remind me to thank Yolanda _____ all the hard work she put into the project.

16. Many people recoil _____ overbearing loudmouths.

17. It's difficult to have respect _____ Scott because he is so egotistical and selfish.

18. It was just announced _____ the radio that Ira won the lottery! Can you believe his luck?

19. Sara started a diet today. She's determined to lose her extra weight once and _____ all.

20. Everybody's meeting at the park on Sunday night for a candlelight vigil to <u>pray</u> _____ peace.

21. John Lennon explained that the Beatles chose their name because it <u>alluded</u> _____ an earlier band named Buddy Holly and the Crickets.

THURSDAY

1.   After Lettie betrayed me by revealing my secret to her friends, I <u>crossed</u> her _____ my list of friends.

2. It was <u>good</u> _____ Daniel to drive his grandmother to her bridge game.

3. I'm _____ my <u>worst</u> in the morning before my first cup of coffee.

4. I'm _____ my <u>best</u> after I've had a day off from work and have had a chance to take a long, luxurious nap.

5. Lorena <u>complained</u> _____ her supervisor about a co-worker's racial slurs.

6. The fans in the stadium <u>jeered</u> _____ the tennis player after he showed poor sportsmanship.

7. _____ <u>all means</u>, bring your new girlfriend to the party on Saturday. I can't wait to meet her!

8. Are you _____ <u>favor</u> _____ the new tax cut proposals, or are you opposed to them?

9. Jan has no real job. She just lives <u>day</u> _____ <u>day.</u>

10. _____ <u>time</u> _____ <u>time</u>, I really enjoy an ice cream sundae dripping with hot fudge and whipped cream.

11. My essay was so full of grammatical errors that my teacher is making me <u>do</u> it _____.

12. I bought the wrong book _____ <u>mistake.</u> Now I have to return it to the bookstore.

13. I don't mind _____ the least if Patty and her fiancé come for dinner on Friday night.

14. What holiday do you most look forward _____? For me, it's Thanksgiving.

15. Remind me to thank Yolanda _____ all the hard work she put into the project.

16. Many people recoil _____ overbearing loudmouths.

17. It's difficult to have respect _____ Scott because he is so egotistical and selfish.

18. It was just announced _____ the radio that Ira won the lottery! Can you believe his luck?

19. Sara started a diet today. She's determined to lose her extra weight once and _____ all.

20. Everybody's meeting at the park on Sunday night for a candlelight vigil to pray _____ peace.

21. John Lennon explained that the Beatles chose their name because it alluded _____ an earlier band named Buddy Holly and the Crickets.

FRIDAY

1. After Lettie betrayed me by revealing my secret to her friends, I crossed her _____ my list of friends.

2. It was good _____ Daniel to drive his grandmother to her bridge game.

3. I'm _____ my worst in the morning before my first cup of coffee.

4. I'm _____ my best after I've had a day off from work and have had a chance to take a long, luxurious nap.

5. Lorena complained _____ her supervisor about a co-worker's racial slurs.

6. The fans in the stadium <u>jeered</u> _____ the tennis player after he showed poor sportsmanship.

7. _____ <u>all means</u>, bring your new girlfriend to the dinner on Saturday. I can't wait to meet her!

8. Are you _____ <u>favor</u> _____ the new tax cut proposals, or are you opposed to them?

9. Jan has no real job. She just lives <u>day</u> _____ <u>day.</u>

10. _____ <u>time</u> _____ <u>time</u>, I really enjoy an ice cream sundae dripping with hot fudge and whipped cream.

11. My essay was so full of grammatical errors that my teacher is making me <u>do</u> it _____.

12. I bought the wrong book _____ <u>mistake</u>. Now I have to return it to the bookstore.

13. I don't mind _____ <u>the least</u> if Patty and her fiancé come for dinner on Friday night.

14. What holiday do you most <u>look forward</u> _____? For me, it's Thanksgiving.

15. Remind me to <u>thank</u> Yolanda _____ all the hard work she put into the project.

16. Many people <u>recoil</u> _____ overbearing loudmouths.

17. It's difficult to have <u>respect</u> _____ Scott because he is so egotistical and selfish.

18. It was just announced _____ <u>the radio</u> that Ira won the lottery! Can you believe his luck?

19. Sara started a diet today. She's determined to lose her extra weight <u>once and</u> _____ <u>all</u>.

20. Everybody's meeting at the park on Sunday night for a candlelight vigil to <u>pray</u> _____ peace.

21. John Lennon explained that the Beatles chose their name because it <u>alluded</u> _____ an earlier band named Buddy Holly and the Crickets.

DISCUSSION

1. At what time of day are you <u>at your worst</u>? Why? Describe what you are like.

2. At what time of day are you <u>at your best</u>? Why? Describe what you are like.

3. Are you <u>in favor of</u> legalizing marijuana? Why? Why not?

4. What personality traits do you <u>recoil from</u>?

5. What's your favorite show <u>on television</u>? (In this country and in your country).

REVIEW WEEKS 9-12

WEEK 9

1. I need to look _____ my notes one last time before the exam tomorrow.

2. The American public is increasingly skeptical _____ its politicians.

3. Because Juan was always curious _____ life in the future, when he became terminally ill, he paid to have his body frozen at death so that he could eventually be brought back to life.

4. Benjamin Franklin is very famous _____ his scientific experiments with electricity.

5. Maria is having trouble deciding _____ which dress she should wear to the prom.

6. Mr. Martinelli remembers that his teachers were prejudiced _____ minorities when he was in school in the 1940's.

7. I used to smoke two packs of cigarettes a day, but that was _____ the past.

8. Because Norman is intent _____ getting a promotion, he puts in a lot of overtime.

9. American school children have to learn the Pledge of Allegiance _____ heart when they are in 1st grade.

10. Marcy wastes so much money _____ manicures and pedicures. Don't you think she'd be better using that money to pay off her credit cards?

11. I've never traveled outside of the USA. In fact, my travel experience has been <u>confined</u> _____ southern California.

12. Sylvia's hairstyle is hopelessly <u>out</u> _____ <u>date</u>. She's worn that style since 1951.

13. It's going to take five trips to <u>carry</u> _____ all of the trash from last night's party.

14. Teri deserves to "Ace" her math class <u>after</u> <u>all</u> _____ the time she's spent studying.

15. As Luis sat on the jury, he became more and more <u>convinced</u> _____ the accused's innocence.

16. There can be a <u>maximum</u> _____ only twenty people in this elevator.

17. To be <u>eligible</u> _____ this job, the applicant must have at least five years experience.

18. The picnic is planned for Sunday, so let's <u>hope</u> _____ warm weather.

19. It's impossible to spend time with Stanley. All he does is <u>boast</u> _____ his son's accomplishments.

20. Don't <u>boast</u> _____ your colleagues about your job promotion. It'll make them feel jealous.

21. I've been <u>wrestling</u> _____ a dilemma: should I quit my job at the store to pursue my singing career or is that just foolish?

WEEK 10

1. Cindy was <u>ashamed</u> _____ the loud voice that her father used when he was in public.

2. John always <u>shows</u> _____ late to office meetings. The boss is starting to get annoyed.

3. If Roget wants to <u>succeed</u> _____ the piano, he's going to have to practice a lot more than he does presently.

4. Have you ever seen the film "The Shawshank Redemption"? It's the story of one man's <u>escape</u> _____ prison.

5. I wish they would <u>turn</u> _____ the heat in the theater. I'm freezing!

6. Children are usually taught to <u>beware</u> _____ strangers. This advice is especially good in today's dangerous world.

7. As Shelly became more and more depressed, she increasingly <u>withdrew</u> _____ social activities and friends.

8. How many days have you been <u>absent</u> _____ class? It seems as though you've been gone forever!

9. Timothy is so <u>careless</u> _____ what he says in front of other people. Just yesterday, he told everyone my deepest secret!

10. _____ <u>long</u>, you will have finished your program and will be a dental hygienist. Congratulations!

11. Look at the necklace. It's completely <u>composed</u> _____ sea shells.

12. Mrs. Stasick is the meanest teacher I've ever had. She <u>sneers</u> _____ all of the students, making us feel inferior and stupid. I don't understand why she continues to teach.

13. Can you believe that Annalie's wedding gown was completely sewn _____ <u>hand</u>?

14. I <u>gave</u> _____ temptation and ate an entire box of choco-late. Yum!

15. For me, the beach is always <u>preferable</u> _____ the mountains. How about for you?

16. Stephen is so <u>enthusiastic</u> _____ the Yankees that he knows every possible statistic about the team and its players.

17. Because of the construction, they had to <u>detour</u> _____ the main highway.

18. Val's always been <u>jealous</u> _____ Susan's jet black hair, while Susan has always hated it.

19. It looked as though that car smacked into the mailbox _____ <u>purpose</u>.

20. <u>All</u> _____ <u>a sudden</u> the beautiful sky was replaced by a dark, threatening one.

21. _____ <u>the most part</u>, this has been the most wonderful vacation of my life.

WEEK 11

1. Why is Miguel always _____ such <u>a hurry</u>?

2. Unfortunately, we <u>based</u> our decision _____ information that proved to be untrue.

3. Many people believe that society should <u>do away</u> _____ the death penalty.

4. That professor is so boring. Her lectures <u>go</u> _____ and _____.

5. I hope that Mr. Rafferty doesn't <u>call</u> _____ me today because I didn't have time to complete my homework.

6. I don't <u>feel</u> <u>sorry</u> _____ for Alex. I know he lost his job, but he was fired because he was lazy and had a terrible attitude.

7. Eve explained how <u>sorry</u> she was _____ missing the party last night, but she had to work late into the night.

8. Let's go out for dinner <u>instead</u> _____ eating at home tonight.

9. It's time for the Smiths to <u>get rid</u> _____ their old jalopy, don't you think? It's not dependable anymore.

10. It was <u>considerate</u> _____ Pablo to invite Teresa to his birthday party since she's new in town and knows very few people.

11. <u>Watch out</u> _____ jelly fish at the beach in August. Their sting really hurts.

12. I'll meet you on the corner of Main and Maple at 5:00. <u>Watch</u> _____ me.

13. The child seat law may be inconvenient, but it was <u>passed</u> _____ the safety of children.

14. Emily and Eric <u>agree</u> _____ absolutely nothing. How do they stay married?

15. Judy and Mike don't <u>agree</u> _____ each other about politics – she's a Democrat and he's a Republican.

16. I've been <u>hooked</u> _____ reading for as long as I can remember.

17. Why did the city <u>tear</u> _____ the Cove Theater? I loved that old building!

18. Whenever I'm sad, I <u>cheer</u> <u>myself</u> _____ by sitting on my couch with a great big bowl of gooey chocolate ice cream and a spoon. Then, I happily watch one of my favorite old movies.

19. It's <u>evident</u> _____ Ali's behavior that he isn't interested in Mariline anymore.

20. Don't forget to <u>turn</u> _____ your essay tomorrow. If it's late, you'll have an entire letter grade deducted.

21. A great job <u>combines</u> interesting work _____ good pay and good working conditions.

WEEK 12

1. After Lettie betrayed me by revealing my secret to her friends, I <u>crossed</u> her _____ my list of friends.

2. It was <u>good</u> _____ Daniel to drive his grandmother to her bridge game.

3. I'm _____ my <u>worst</u> in the morning before my first cup of coffee.

4. I'm _____ my <u>best</u> after I've had a day off from work and have had a chance to take a long, luxurious nap.

5. Lorena <u>complained</u> _____ her supervisor about a co-worker's racial slurs.

6. The fans in the stadium <u>jeered</u> _____ the tennis player after he showed poor sportsmanship.

7. _____ <u>all means</u>, bring your new girlfriend to the party on Saturday. I can't wait to meet her!

8. Are you _____ <u>favor</u> _____ the new tax cut proposals, or are you opposed to them?

9. Jan has no real job. She just lives <u>day</u> _____ <u>day.</u>

10. _____ <u>time</u> _____ <u>time</u>, I really enjoy an ice cream sundae dripping with hot fudge and whipped cream.

11. My essay was so full of grammatical errors that my teacher is making me <u>do</u> it _____.

12. I bought the wrong book _____ <u>mistake</u>. Now I have to return it to the bookstore.

13. I don't mind _____ <u>the least</u> if Patty and her fiancé come for dinner on Friday night.

14. What holiday do you most <u>look forward</u> _____? For me, it's Thanksgiving.

15. Remind me to <u>thank</u> Yolanda _____ all the hard work she put into the project.

16. Many people <u>recoil</u> _____ overbearing loudmouths.

17. It's difficult to have <u>respect</u> _____ Scott because he is so egotistical and selfish.

18. It was just announced _____ <u>the radio</u> that Ira won the lottery! Can you believe his luck?

19. Sara started a diet today. She's determined to lose her extra weight <u>once and</u> _____ <u>all</u>.

20. Everybody's meeting at the park on Sunday night for a candlelight vigil to <u>pray</u> _____ peace.

21. John Lennon explained that the Beatles chose their name because it <u>alluded</u> _____ an earlier band named Buddy Holly and the Crickets.

WEEK 13

MONDAY

1. This essay is <u>typical</u> _____ the kind of work that Miguel always submits.

2. My English teacher is <u>demanding</u> three research papers _____ each student this term. I think that's too much.

3. Cecily seemed <u>oblivious</u> _____ the insulting remark that Tom made.

4. The tomatoes looked ripe, but when I bit into one, it was <u>devoid</u> _____ any flavor.

5. _____ <u>the end</u>, Susan's parents were right to worry about her: she was depressed.

6. The librarian kindly <u>suggested</u> _____ the rowdy students that they be quiet.

7. After studying for an entire year, Nora felt confident about her English _____ <u>the first time</u> in her life.

TUESDAY

1. This essay is <u>typical</u> _____ the kind of work that Miguel always submits.

2. My English teacher is <u>demanding</u> three research papers _____ each student this term. I think that's too much.

3. Cecily seemed <u>oblivious</u> _____ the insulting remark that Tom made.

4. The tomatoes looked ripe, but when I bit into one, it was <u>devoid</u> _____ any flavor.

5. _____ <u>the end</u>, Susan's parents were right to worry about her: she was depressed.

6. The librarian kindly <u>suggested</u> _____ the rowdy students that they be quiet.

7. After studying for an entire year, Nora felt confident about her English _____ <u>the first time</u> in her life.

8. Please put whipped cream and a cherry _____ <u>top</u> _____ my ice cream.

9. Yu is hoping that working 20 hours a week won't <u>interfere</u> too much _____ her studies.

10. Doesn't Pedro <u>remind</u> you _____ his father?

11. _____ <u>contrast</u> _____ his sister who loves to stay at home and read, Robert is an extrovert who prefers to be out with friends.

12. Mr. Smithers won't <u>stand</u> _____ any disrespect from his employees.

13. The students in this class <u>come</u> _____ a total of 25 countries.

14. Why does Rachel <u>persist</u> _____ telling lies? Nobody believes a word she says!

WEDNESDAY

1. This essay is <u>typical</u> _____ the kind of work that Miguel always submits.

2. My English teacher is <u>demanding</u> three research papers _____ each student this term. I think that's too much.

3. Cecily seemed <u>oblivious</u> _____ the insulting remark that Tom made.

4. The tomatoes looked ripe, but when I bit into one, it was <u>devoid</u> _____ any flavor.

5. _____ the end, Susan's parents were right to worry about her: she was depressed.

6. The librarian kindly suggested _____ the rowdy students that they be quiet.

7. After studying for an entire year, Nora felt confident about her English _____ the first time in her life.

8. Please put whipped cream and a cherry _____ top _____ my ice cream.

9. Yu is hoping that working 20 hours a week won't interfere too much _____ her studies.

10. Doesn't Pedro remind you _____ his father?

11. _____ contrast _____ his sister who loves to stay at home and read, Robert is an extrovert who prefers to be out with friends.

12. Mr. Smithers won't stand _____ any disrespect from his employees.

13. The students in this class come _____ a total of 25 countries.

14. Why does Rachel persist _____ telling lies? Nobody believes a word she says!

15. Because Melissa never reads a newspaper, she is completely ignorant _____ what is occurring in the world.

16. Juan is not very happy _____ his new job because he is given very little responsibility.

17. Tomatoes were originally exported _____ Italy from North America.

18. Now, countries from around the world import tomato sauce _____ Italy.

19. Can you believe that I ran _____ Teddy yesterday? I haven't seen him since high school.

20. The President's popularity has <u>increased</u> _____ 40% _____ 60% since last January.

21. I know that eating a gooey, hot fudge sundae several times a week is <u>detrimental</u> _____ my health, but what's an ice-cream lover to do?

THURSDAY

1. This essay is <u>typical</u> _____ the kind of work that Miguel always submits.

2. My English teacher is <u>demanding</u> three research papers _____ each student this term. I think that's too much.

3. Cecily seemed <u>oblivious</u> _____ the insulting remark that Tom made.

4. The tomatoes looked ripe, but when I bit into one, it was <u>devoid</u> _____ any flavor.

5. _____ <u>the end</u>, Susan's parents were right to worry about her: she was depressed.

6. The librarian kindly <u>suggested</u> _____ the rowdy students that they be quiet.

7. After studying for an entire year, Nora felt confident about her English _____ <u>the first time</u> in her life.

8. Please put whipped cream and a cherry _____ <u>top</u> _____ my ice cream.

9. Yu is hoping that working 20 hours a week won't <u>interfere</u> too much _____ her studies.

10. Doesn't Pedro <u>remind</u> you _____ his father?

11. _____ <u>contrast</u> _____ his sister who loves to stay at home and read, Robert is an extrovert who prefers to be out with friends.

12. Mr. Smithers won't <u>stand</u> _____ any disrespect from his employees.

13. The students in this class <u>come</u> _____ a total of 25 countries.

14. Why does Rachel <u>persist</u> _____ telling lies? Nobody believes a word she says!

15. Because Melissa never reads a newspaper, she is completely <u>ignorant</u> _____ what is occurring in the world.

16. Juan is not very <u>happy</u> _____ his new job because he is given very little responsibility.

17. Tomatoes were originally <u>exported</u> _____ Italy from North America.

18. Now, countries from around the world <u>import</u> tomato sauce _____ Italy.

19. Can you believe that I <u>ran</u> _____ Teddy yesterday? I haven't seen him since high school.

20. The President's popularity has <u>increased</u> _____ 40% _____ 60% since last January.

21. I know that eating a gooey, hot fudge sundae several times a week is <u>detrimental</u> _____ my health, but what's an ice-cream lover to do?

FRIDAY

1. This essay is <u>typical</u> _____ the kind of work that Miguel always submits.

2. My English teacher is <u>demanding</u> three research papers _____ each student this term. I think that's too much.

3. Cecily seemed <u>oblivious</u> _____ the insulting remark that Tom made.

4. The tomatoes looked ripe, but when I bit into one, it was <u>devoid</u> _____ any flavor.

5. _____ the end, Susan's parents were right to worry about her: she was depressed.

6. The librarian kindly <u>suggested</u> _____ the rowdy students that they be quiet.

7. After studying for an entire year, Nora felt confident about her English _____ <u>the first time</u> in her life.

8. Please put whipped cream and a cherry _____ <u>top</u> _____ my ice cream.

9. Yu is hoping that working 20 hours a week won't <u>interfere</u> too much _____ her studies.

10. Doesn't Pedro <u>remind</u> you _____ his father?

11. _____ <u>contrast</u> _____ his sister who loves to stay at home and read, Robert is an extrovert who prefers to be out with friends.

12. Mr. Smithers won't <u>stand</u> _____ any disrespect from his employees.

13. The students in this class <u>come</u> _____ a total of 25 countries.

14. Why does Rachel <u>persist</u> _____ telling lies? Nobody believes a word she says!

15. Because Melissa never reads a newspaper, she is completely <u>ignorant</u> _____ what is occurring in the world.

16. Juan is not very <u>happy</u> _____ his new job because he is given very little responsibility.

17. Tomatoes were originally <u>exported</u> _____ Italy from North America.

18. Now, countries from around the world <u>import</u> tomato sauce _____ Italy.

19. Can you believe that I <u>ran</u> _____ Teddy yesterday? I haven't seen him since high school.

20. The President's popularity has <u>increased</u> _____ 40% _____ 60% since last January.

21. I know that eating a gooey, hot fudge sundae several times a week is <u>detrimental</u> _____ my health, but what's an ice-cream lover to do?

DISCUSSION

1. Name three things about your life that you are really <u>happy with</u>. Name one or more thing that you would like to change.

2. What is<u> exported from</u> your country to other countries around the world?

3. Get up and show your partner on one of the maps in the room exactly where you <u>come from</u>.

4. Do you <u>persist in</u> studying when the work gets hard, or do you get frustrated and give up?

5. What weather is <u>typical of</u> the city that you come from?

WEEK 14

MONDAY

1. The hotel room was filthy, but since it was already midnight, we decided that it was <u>adequate</u> _____ one night.

2. Police officers must <u>advise</u> people being arrested _____ their *Miranda* rights.

3. You won't believe what happened to me _____ <u>the way</u> to church this morning!

4. I was wrong. _____ <u>fact</u>, Jim is celebrating his 50th birthday.

5. <u>Contrary</u> _____ her mother's wishes, Samantha wore all black to the wedding.

6. The teacher <u>suspected</u> the class _____ cheating on her exams, so she devised an elaborate test to catch them.

7. The teacher was <u>encouraged</u> _____ the classes' progress in reading.

TUESDAY

1. The hotel room was filthy, but since it was already midnight, we decided that it was <u>adequate</u> _____ one night.

2. Police officers must <u>advise</u> people being arrested _____ their *Miranda* rights.

3. You won't believe what happened to me _____ <u>the way</u> to church this morning!

4. I was wrong. _____ <u>fact</u>, Jim is celebrating his 50th birthday.

5. <u>Contrary</u> _____ her mother's wishes, Samantha wore all black to the wedding.

6. The teacher <u>suspected</u> the class _____ cheating on her exams, so she devised an elaborate test to catch them.

7. The teacher was <u>encouraged</u> _____ the classes' progress in reading.

8. Don't forget to <u>put</u> _____ the pots and pans when you are done baking.

9. Mrs. Smith fell into a funk when her husband died. She just can't imagine <u>going</u> _____ _____ him.

10. When you're at the supermarket, <u>inquire</u> _____ job openings. I hear they pay well.

11. When Tom was complaining about Professor Brooks, he was <u>referring</u> _____ the professor who teaches history – not the one who teaches art history.

12. Sally and Tom are leaving next month to <u>embark</u> _____ a trip around the world.

13. Lorena <u>worked</u> _____ her master's thesis for over two years.

14. Why are you so <u>opposed</u> _____ my becoming an actress? It seems like such an exciting way to live my life.

WEDNESDAY

1. The hotel room was filthy, but since it was already midnight, we decided that it was <u>adequate</u> _____ one night.

2. Police officers must <u>advise</u> people being arrested _____ their *Miranda* rights.

3. You won't believe what happened to me _____ <u>the way</u> to church this morning!

4. I was wrong. _____ <u>fact</u>, Jim is celebrating his 50th birthday.

5. <u>Contrary</u> _____ her mother's wishes, Samantha wore all black to the wedding.

6. The teacher <u>suspected</u> the class _____ cheating on her exams, so she devised an elaborate test to catch them.

7. The teacher was <u>encouraged</u> _____ the classes' progress in reading.

8. Don't forget to <u>put</u> _____ the pots and pans when you are done baking.

9. Mrs. Smith fell into a funk when her husband died. She just can't imagine <u>going</u> _____ _____ him.

10. When you're at the supermarket, <u>inquire</u> _____ job openings. I hear they pay well.

11. When Tom was complaining about Professor Brooks, he was <u>referring</u> _____ the professor who teaches history – not the one who teaches art history.

12. Sally and Tom are leaving next month to <u>embark</u> _____ a trip around the world.

13. Lorena <u>worked</u> _____ her master's thesis for over two years.

14. Why are you so <u>opposed</u> _____ my becoming an actress? It seems like such an exciting way to live my life.

15. Norman bought that old jalopy _____ <u>the purpose</u> _____ working on it until it is completely restored.

16. When the teacher caught her student cheating on the final examination, she was so angry that she <u>tore</u> the test paper _____.

17. Exhausted from work, Bridget and Howard couldn't wait to <u>get away</u> _____ the city for a weekend.

18. Nancy is flying east next week to <u>attend</u> _____ her mother, who injured her hip when she slipped on the ice.

19. After not having spoken for over twenty years, the Talbot brothers finally <u>got together</u> _____ each other last weekend.

20. Do you <u>take</u> _____ your mother or your father in personality?

21. Joanna called to <u>apologize</u> _____ standing me up last night. It seems that her car broke down and her cell phone wasn't working.

THURSDAY

1. The hotel room was filthy, but since it was already midnight, we decided that it was <u>adequate</u> _____ one night.

2. Police officers must <u>advise</u> people being arrested _____ their *Miranda* rights.

3. You won't believe what happened to me _____ <u>the way</u> to church this morning!

4. I was wrong. _____ <u>fact</u>, Jim is celebrating his 50th birthday.

5. <u>Contrary</u> _____ her mother's wishes, Samantha wore all black to the wedding.

6. The teacher <u>suspected</u> the class _____ cheating on her exams, so she devised an elaborate test to catch them.

7. The teacher was <u>encouraged</u> _____ the classes' progress in reading.

8. Don't forget to <u>put</u> _____ the pots and pans when you are done baking.

9. Mrs. Smith fell into a funk when her husband died. She just can't imagine <u>going</u> _____ _____ him.

10. When you're at the supermarket, <u>inquire</u> _____ job openings. I hear they pay well.

11. When Tom was complaining about Professor Brooks, he was <u>referring</u> _____ the professor who teaches history – not the one who teaches art history.

12. Sally and Tom are leaving next month to <u>embark</u> _____ a trip around the world.

13. Lorena <u>worked</u> _____ her master's thesis for over two years.

14. Why are you so <u>opposed</u> _____ my becoming an actress? It seems like such an exciting way to live my life.

15. Norman bought that old jalopy _____ <u>the purpose</u> working on it until it is completely restored.

16. When the teacher caught her student cheating on the final examination, she was so angry that she <u>tore</u> the test paper _____.

17. Exhausted from work, Bridget and Howard couldn't wait to <u>get away</u> _____ the city for a weekend.

18. Nancy is flying east next week to <u>attend</u> _____ her mother, who injured her hip when she slipped on the ice.

19. After not having spoken for over twenty years, the Talbot brothers finally <u>got</u> <u>together</u> _____ each other last weekend.

20. Do you <u>take</u> _____ your mother or your father in personality?

21. Joanna called to <u>apologize</u> _____ standing me up last night. It seems that her car broke down and her cell phone wasn't working.

FRIDAY

1. The hotel room was filthy, but since it was already midnight, we decided that it was <u>adequate</u> _____ one night.

2. Police officers must <u>advise</u> people being arrested _____ their *Miranda* rights.

3. You won't believe what happened to me _____ <u>the way</u> to church this morning!

4. I was wrong. _____ <u>fact</u>, Jim is celebrating his 50ᵗʰ birthday.

5. <u>Contrary</u> _____ her mother's wishes, Samantha wore all black to the wedding.

6. The teacher <u>suspected</u> the class _____ cheating on her exams, so she devised an elaborate test to catch them.

7. The teacher was <u>encouraged</u> _____ the classes' progress in reading.

8. Don't forget to <u>put</u> _____ the pots and pans when you are done baking.

9. Mrs. Smith fell into a funk when her husband died. She just can't imagine <u>going</u> _____ _____ him.

10. When you're at the supermarket, <u>inquire</u> _____ job openings. I hear they pay well.

11. When Tom was complaining about Professor Brooks, he was <u>referring</u> _____ the professor who teaches history – not the one who teaches art history.

12. Sally and Tom are leaving next month to <u>embark</u> _____ a trip around the world.

13. Lorena <u>worked</u> _____ her master's thesis for over two years.

14. Why are you so <u>opposed</u> _____ my becoming an actress? It seems like such an exciting way to live my life.

15. Norman bought that old jalopy _____ <u>the purpose</u> _____ working on it until it is completely restored.

16. When the teacher caught her student cheating on the final examination, she was so angry that she <u>tore</u> the test paper _____.

17. Exhausted from work, Bridget and Howard couldn't wait to <u>get away</u> _____ the city for a weekend.

18. Nancy is flying east next week to <u>attend</u> _____ her mother, who injured her hip when she slipped on the ice.

19. After not having spoken for over twenty years, the Talbot brothers finally <u>got together</u> _____ each other last weekend.

20. Do you <u>take</u> _____ your mother or your father in personality?

21. Joanna called to <u>apologize</u> _____ standing me up last night. It seems that her car broke down and her cell phone wasn't working.

DISCUSSION

1. Are you <u>in favor of</u> or <u>opposed to</u> abortion? Why?

2. If you could <u>get away from</u> home for "a long weekend," where would you go?

3. When was the last time your entire family <u>got together with</u> each other? What did you do? When do you think you will all see each other again?

4. Do you <u>take after</u> you mother or your father in appearance? In personality?

5. Do you always <u>put</u> your clothes <u>away</u> at night, or do you leave them lying all over the room?

WEEK 15

MONDAY

1. Are you <u>acquainted</u> _____with_____ Joe's friends from school?

2. Trying to <u>keep up</u> _____with_____ a baby is absolutely exhausting.

3. It was cruel of Tony to <u>laugh</u> _____ the woman when she slipped and fell on her face.

4. Because we really care for and support each other, our class <u>laughed</u> __with__ love at Julie when she giggled uncontrollably during her presentation.

5. I think that tiny, furry kittens are the <u>epitome</u> _____of_____ cuteness.

6. How is a student supposed to <u>obtain</u> knowledge _____from_____ this teacher when she doesn't know much about her subject matter?

7. Lettie's bed is <u>covered</u> _____by / with_____ the most beautiful comforter that I have ever seen.

TUESDAY

1. Are you <u>acquainted</u> _____ Joe's friends from school?

2. Trying to <u>keep up</u> _____ a baby is absolutely exhausting.

3. It was cruel of Tony to <u>laugh</u> _____ the woman when she slipped and fell on her face.

4. Because we really care for and support each other, our class <u>laughed</u> _____ love at Julie when she giggled uncontrollably during her presentation.

5. I think that tiny, furry kittens are the <u>epitome</u> _____ cuteness.

6. How is a student supposed to <u>obtain</u> knowledge _____ this teacher when she doesn't know much about her subject matter?

7. Lettie's bed is <u>covered</u> _____ the most beautiful comforter that I have ever seen.

8. Can you <u>cover</u> _____ me at the meeting today? I have to make an emergency visit to the dentist.

9. How was it possible for Veronica to <u>run</u> _____ _____ gas? You'd think she would have checked her gas gauge before setting out on the trip.

10. Jason declared himself <u>independent</u> _____ his parents the minute he turned eighteen by immediately moving into his own apartment.

11. I wish my husband had <u>pointed</u> _____ that I had spinach trapped in my teeth before I had my picture taken.

12. General Adams just <u>retired</u> _____ the military after 40 years of service.

13. Are these directions <u>clear</u> _____ you? I'm lost.

14. Nancy made a generous contribution to the American Heart Association _____ <u>the name</u> _____ her uncle, Ed.

WEDNESDAY

1. Are you <u>acquainted</u> _____ Joe's friends from school?

2. Trying to <u>keep up</u> _____ a baby is absolutely exhausting.

3. It was cruel of Tony to <u>laugh</u> _____ the woman when she slipped and fell on her face.

4. Because we really care for and support each other, our class <u>laughed</u> _____ love at Julie when she giggled uncontrollably during her presentation.

5. I think that tiny, furry kittens are the <u>epitome</u> _____ cuteness.

6. How is a student supposed to <u>obtain</u> knowledge _____ this teacher when she doesn't know much about her subject matter?

7. Lettie's bed is <u>covered</u> _____ the most beautiful comforter that I have ever seen.

8. Can you <u>cover</u> _____ me at the meeting today? I have to make an emergency visit to the dentist.

9. How was it possible for Veronica to <u>run</u> _____ _____ gas? You'd think she would have checked her gas gauge before setting out on the trip.

10. Jason declared himself <u>independent</u> _____ his parents the minute he turned eighteen by immediately moving into his own apartment.

11. I wish my husband had <u>pointed</u> _____ that I had spinach trapped in my teeth before I had my picture taken.

12. General Adams just <u>retired</u> _____ the military after 40 years of service.

13. Are these directions <u>clear</u> _____ you? I'm lost.

14. Nancy made a generous contribution to the American Heart Association _____ <u>the name</u> _____ her uncle, Ed.

15. Although my alarm clock failed to go off this morning, I made it to the train station <u>just</u> _____ <u>time</u> to make my train.

16. This dress is much too expensive for my budget, but I simply have to <u>try</u> it _____.

17. Do you think it is <u>appropriate</u> _____ a ten-year-old girl to wear make-up?

18. While Suzie <u>teared</u> _____ watching "Titanic," I laughed my head off.

19. Merrie no longer has <u>faith</u> _____ Wayne and is, therefore, divorcing him.

20. <u>Look out</u> _____ holes in the sidewalk; my mother fell into one and broke her hip.

21. Are you going to <u>vote</u> _____ the incumbent senator or for his opponent?

THURSDAY

1. Are you <u>acquainted</u> _____with_____ Joe's friends from school?

2. Trying to <u>keep up</u> _____with_____ a baby is absolutely exhausting.

3. It was cruel of Tony to <u>laugh</u> _____at_____ the woman when she slipped and fell on her face.

4. Because we really care for and support each other, our class <u>laughed</u> _____with_____ love at Julie when she giggled uncontrollably during her presentation.

5.   I think that tiny, furry kittens are the <u>epitome</u> _____of_____ cuteness.

6. How is a student supposed to <u>obtain</u> knowledge _____from_____ this teacher when she doesn't know much about her subject matter?

7. Lettie's bed is <u>covered</u> _____by / with_____ the most beautiful comforter that I have ever seen.

8. Can you <u>cover</u> _____for_____ me at the meeting today? I have to make an emergency visit to the dentist.

9. How was it possible for Veronica to <u>run</u> _____out_____ _____of_____ gas? You'd think she would have checked her gas gauge before setting out on the trip.

10.   Jason declared himself <u>independent</u> _____of_____ his parents the minute he turned eighteen by immediately moving into his own apartment.

11. I wish my husband had <u>pointed</u> _____out_____ that I had spinach trapped in my teeth before I had my picture taken.

12. General Adams just <u>retired</u> _____from_____ the military after 40 years of service.

13. Are these directions <u>clear</u> _____to_____ you? I'm lost.

14. Nancy made a generous contribution to the American Heart Association _____in_____ <u>the name</u> _____of_____ her uncle, Ed.

15. Although my alarm clock failed to go off this morning, I made it to the train station <u>just</u> _____in/on_____ <u>time</u> to make my train.

16. This dress is much too expensive for my budget, but I simply have to <u>try</u> it _____on_____ .

17. Do you think it is <u>appropriate</u> _____for_____ a ten-year-old girl to wear make-up?

18. While Suzie <u>teared</u> _____up_____ watching "Titanic," I laughed my head off.

19. Merrie no longer has <u>faith</u> _____in_____ Wayne and is, therefore, divorcing him.

20. <u>Look out</u> _____for_____ holes in the sidewalk; my mother fell into one and broke her hip.

21. Are you going to <u>vote</u> _____for_____ the incumbent senator or for his opponent?

FRIDAY

1. Are you <u>acquainted</u> _____ Joe's friends from school?

2. Trying to <u>keep up</u> _____ a baby is absolutely exhausting.

3. It was cruel of Tony to <u>laugh</u> _____ the woman when she slipped and fell on her face.

4. Because we really care for and support each other, our class <u>laughed</u> _____ love at Julie when she giggled uncontrollably during her presentation.

5. I think that tiny, furry kittens are the <u>epitome</u> _____ cuteness.

6. How is a student supposed to <u>obtain</u> knowledge _____ this teacher when she doesn't know much about her subject matter?

7. Lettie's bed is <u>covered</u> _____ the most beautiful comforter that I have ever seen.

8. Can you <u>cover</u> _____ me at the meeting today? I have to make an emergency visit to the dentist.

9. How was it possible for Veronica to <u>run</u> _____ _____ gas? You'd think she would have checked her gas gauge before setting out on the trip.

10. Jason declared himself <u>independent</u> _____ his parents the minute he turned eighteen by immediately moving into his own apartment.

11. I wish my husband had <u>pointed</u> _____ that I had spinach trapped in my teeth before I had my picture taken.

12. General Adams just <u>retired</u> _____ the military after 40 years of service.

13. Are these directions <u>clear</u> _____ you? I'm lost.

14. Nancy made a generous contribution to the American Heart Association _____ <u>the name</u> _____ her uncle, Ed.

15. Although my alarm clock failed to go off this morning, I made it to the train station <u>just</u> _____ <u>time</u> to make my train.

16. This dress is much too expensive for my budget, but I simply have to <u>try</u> it _____.

17. Do you think it is <u>appropriate</u> _____ a ten-year-old girl to wear make-up?

18. While Suzie <u>teared</u> _____ watching "Titanic," I laughed my head off.

19. Merrie no longer has <u>faith</u> _____ Wayne and is, therefore, divorcing him.

20. <u>Look out</u> _____ holes in the sidewalk; my mother fell into one and broke her hip.

21. Are you going to <u>vote</u> _____ the incumbent senator or for his opponent?

DISCUSSION

1. Are you <u>acquainted with</u> anyone who is famous? Who?

2. Which movie always makes you <u>tear up</u>?

3. How old do you think you'll be when you <u>retire from</u> your career? What do you think you would like to do when you retire?

4. Have you ever <u>run out of</u> gas? When? What happened?

5. Can you remember an embarrassing moment when people <u>laughed at</u> you?

WEEK 16

MONDAY

1. The book <u>East of Eden</u> had such a profound <u>effect</u> _____ Molly that she decided to become a writer.

2. I borrowed my mother-in-law's pearls and lost them _____ <u>accident</u>. How am I going to tell her?

3. Can you think of a good excuse to <u>get</u> Santiago _____ _____ his dreaded blind date?

4. Maria has <u>dreamed</u> _____ being a singer since she was a small child.

5. Be sure to <u>compliment</u> Scott _____ his new haircut. He's very sensitive about it.

6. No matter how hard she tries, Andrea finds it impossible to <u>get along</u> _____ her boss.

7. Come on over Friday night and we'll spend the evening eating, drinking, and <u>gossiping</u> _____ everyone at work.

TUESDAY

1. The book <u>East of Eden</u> had such a profound <u>effect</u> _____ Molly that she decided to become a writer.

2. I borrowed my mother-in-law's pearls and lost them _____ <u>accident</u>. How am I going to tell her?

3. Can you think of a good excuse to <u>get</u> Santiago _____ _____ his dreaded blind date?

4. Maria has <u>dreamed</u> _____ being a singer since she was a small child.

5. Be sure to <u>compliment</u> Scott _____ his new haircut. He's very sensitive about it.

6. No matter how hard she tries, Andrea finds it impossible to <u>get along</u> _____ her boss.

7. Come on over Friday night and we'll spend the evening eating, drinking, and <u>gossiping</u> _____ everyone at work.

8. No matter how hard I study, I never feel <u>prepared</u> _____ my math exams.

9. Help!!! The kitchen is _____ <u>fire</u>.

10. Martin Luther King lived his life <u>fighting</u> _____ racial equality.

11. This school never has <u>an</u> adequate <u>supply</u> _____ writing paper.

12. I think that each class should be <u>supplied</u> _____ enough paper to last a year.

13. When asked if he is only dating Nora, Henri answered, "_____ <u>a way</u>." What does that mean?

14. Are you <u>positive</u> _____ your answer because I think you're wrong.

WEDNESDAY

1. The book <u>East of Eden</u> had such a profound <u>effect</u> _____ Molly that she decided to become a writer.

2. I borrowed my mother-in-law's pearls and lost them _____ <u>accident</u>. How am I going to tell her?

3. Can you think of a good excuse to <u>get</u> Santiago _____ _____ his dreaded blind date?

4. Maria has <u>dreamed</u> _____ being a singer since she was a small child.

5. Be sure to <u>compliment</u> Scott _____ his new haircut. He's very sensitive about it.

6. No matter how hard she tries, Andrea finds it impossible to <u>get along</u> _____ her boss.

7. Come on over Friday night and we'll spend the evening eating, drinking, and <u>gossiping</u> _____ everyone at work.

8. No matter how hard I study, I never feel <u>prepared</u> _____ my math exams.

9. Help!!! The kitchen is _____ <u>fire</u>.

10. Martin Luther King lived his life <u>fighting</u> _____ racial equality.

11. This school never has <u>an</u> adequate <u>supply</u> _____ writing paper.

12. I think that each class should be <u>supplied</u> _____ enough paper to last a year.

13. When asked if he is only dating Nora, Henri answered, "_____ <u>a way</u>." What does that mean?

14. Are you <u>positive</u> _____ your answer because I think you're wrong.

15. Do you really think that one detergent is <u>inferior</u> _____ another, or do you think that they're all just about the same?

16. It's the dream of people around the world to be <u>safe</u> _____ violence.

17. Albert Einstein has long been <u>thought</u> _____ as one of the greatest minds in history.

18. I spent the entire night <u>thinking</u> _____ Miguel's marriage proposal, and I still don't know how to answer.

19. Are you going to <u>recommend</u> Dennis _____ the promotion?

20. I read a novel by Edith Wharton because my English teacher <u>recommended</u> her work _____ me.

21. Martha takes such <u>delight</u> _____ her grandchildren. It's fun to see.

THURSDAY

1. The book <u>East of Eden</u> had such a profound <u>effect</u> _____ Molly that she decided to become a writer.

2. I borrowed my mother-in-law's pearls and lost them _____ <u>accident</u>. How am I going to tell her?

3. Can you think of a good excuse to <u>get</u> Santiago _____ _____ his dreaded blind date?

4. Maria has <u>dreamed</u> _____ being a singer since she was a small child.

5. Be sure to <u>compliment</u> Scott _____ his new haircut. He's very sensitive about it.

6. No matter how hard she tries, Andrea finds it impossible to <u>get along</u> _____ her boss.

7. Come on over Friday night and we'll spend the evening eating, drinking, and <u>gossiping</u> _____ everyone at work.

8. No matter how hard I study, I never feel <u>prepared</u> _____ my math exams.

9. Help!!! The kitchen is _____ <u>fire</u>.

10. Martin Luther King lived his life <u>fighting</u> _____ racial equality.

11. This school never has <u>an</u> adequate <u>supply</u> _____ writing paper.

12. I think that each class should be <u>supplied</u> _____ enough paper to last a year.

13. When asked if he is only dating Nora, Henri answered, "_____ <u>a way</u>." What does that mean?

14. Are you <u>positive</u> _____ your answer because I think you're wrong.

15. Do you really think that one detergent is <u>inferior</u> _____ another, or do you think that they're all just about the same?

16. It's the dream of people around the world to be <u>safe</u> _____ violence.

17. Albert Einstein has long been <u>thought</u> _____ as one of the greatest minds in history.

18. I spent the entire night <u>thinking</u> _____ Miguel's marriage proposal, and I still don't know how to answer.

19. Are you going to <u>recommend</u> Dennis _____ the promotion?

20. I read a novel by Edith Wharton because my English teacher <u>recommended</u> her work _____ me.

21. Martha takes such <u>delight</u> _____ her grandchildren. It's fun to see.

FRIDAY

1. The book <u>East of Eden</u> had such a profound <u>effect</u> _____ Molly that she decided to become a writer.

2. I borrowed my mother-in-law's pearls and lost them _____ <u>accident</u>. How am I going to tell her?

3. Can you think of a good excuse to <u>get</u> Santiago _____ _____ his dreaded blind date?

4. Maria has <u>dreamed</u> _____ being a singer since she was a small child.

5. Be sure to <u>compliment</u> Scott _____ his new haircut. He's very sensitive about it.

6. No matter how hard she tries, Andrea finds it impossible to <u>get along</u> _____ her boss.

7. Come on over Friday night and we'll spend the evening eating, drinking, and <u>gossiping</u> _____ everyone at work.

8. No matter how hard I study, I never feel <u>prepared</u> _____ my math exams.

9. Help!!! The kitchen is _____ <u>fire</u>.

10. Martin Luther King lived his life <u>fighting</u> _____ racial equality.

11. This school never has <u>an</u> adequate <u>supply</u> _____ writing paper.

12. I think that each class should be <u>supplied</u> _____ enough paper to last a year.

13. When asked if he is only dating Nora, Henri answered, "_____ <u>a way</u>." What does that mean?

14. Are you <u>positive</u> _____ your answer because I think you're wrong.

15. Do you really think that one detergent is <u>inferior</u> _____ another, or do you think that they're all just about the same?

16. It's the dream of people around the world to be <u>safe</u> _____ violence.

17. Albert Einstein has long been <u>thought</u> _____ as one of the greatest minds in history.

18. I spent the entire night <u>thinking</u> _____ Miguel's marriage proposal, and I still don't know how to answer.

19. Are you going to <u>recommend</u> Dennis _____ the promotion?

20. I read a novel by Edith Wharton because my English teacher <u>recommended</u> her work _____ me.

21. Martha takes such <u>delight</u> _____ her grandchildren. It's fun to see.

DISCUSSION

1. What person had a profound <u>effect on</u> you? How did he/she influence you?

2. Would you ever tell a "white lie" to <u>get out of</u> something you didn't want to do, or would you always honor your commitment?

3. Name three people you <u>think of</u> as important to the last century.

4. Name three things/events/people you always <u>(take) delight in</u>.

5. Do you enjoy <u>gossiping about</u> people, or do you think that it is wrong to engage in this activity?

REVIEW WEEKS 13-16

WEEK 13

1. This essay is <u>typical</u> _____ the kind of work that Miguel always submits.

2. My English teacher is <u>demanding</u> three research papers _____ each student this term. I think that's too much.

3. Cecily seemed <u>oblivious</u> _____ the insulting remark that Tom made.

4. The tomatoes looked ripe, but when I bit into one, it was <u>devoid</u> _____ any flavor.

5. _____ <u>the end</u>, Susan's parents were right to worry about her: she was depressed.

6. The librarian kindly <u>suggested</u> _____ the rowdy students that they be quiet.

7. After studying for an entire year, Nora felt confident about her English _____ <u>the first time</u> in her life.

8. Please put whipped cream and a cherry _____ <u>top</u> my ice cream.

9. Yu is hoping that working 20 hours a week won't <u>interfere</u> too much her studies.

10. Doesn't Pedro <u>remind</u> you _____ his father?

11. _____ <u>contrast</u> _____ his sister who loves to stay at home and read, Robert is an extrovert who prefers to be out with friends.

12. Mr. Smithers won't <u>stand</u> _____ any disrespect from his employees.

13. The students in this class <u>come</u> _____ a total of 25 countries.

14. Why does Rachel <u>persist</u> _____ telling lies? Nobody believes a word she says!

15. Because Melissa never reads a newspaper, she is completely <u>ignorant</u> _____ what is occurring in the world.

16. Juan is not very <u>happy</u> _____ his new job because he is given very little responsibility.

17. Tomatoes were originally <u>exported</u> _____ Italy from North America.

18. Now, countries from around the world <u>import</u> tomato sauce _____ Italy.

19. Can you believe that I <u>ran</u> _____ Teddy yesterday? I haven't seen him since high school.

20. The President's popularity has <u>increased</u> _____ 40% _____ 60% since last January.

21. I know that eating a gooey, hot fudge sundae several times a week is <u>detrimental</u> _____ my health, but what's an ice-cream lover to do?

WEEK 14

1. The hotel room was filthy, but since it was already midnight, we decided that it was <u>adequate</u> _____ one night.

2. Police officers must <u>advise</u> people being arrested _____ their *Miranda* rights.

3. You won't believe what happened to me _____ <u>the way</u> to church this morning!

4. I was wrong. _____ <u>fact</u>, Jim is celebrating his 50th birthday.

5. <u>Contrary</u> _____ her mother's wishes, Samantha wore all black to the wedding.

6. The teacher <u>suspected</u> the class _____ cheating on her exams, so she devised an elaborate test to catch them.

7. The teacher was <u>encouraged</u> _____ the classes' progress in reading.

8. Don't forget to <u>put</u> _____ the pots and pans when you are done baking.

9. Mrs. Smith fell into a funk when her husband died. She just can't imagine <u>going</u> _____ _____ him.

10. When you're at the supermarket, <u>inquire</u> _____ job openings. I hear they pay well.

11. When Tom was complaining about Professor Brooks, he was <u>referring</u> _____ the professor who teaches history – not the one who teaches art history.

12. Sally and Tom are leaving next month to <u>embark</u> _____ a trip around the world.

13. Lorena <u>worked</u> _____ her master's thesis for over two years.

14. Why are you so <u>opposed</u> _____ my becoming an actress? It seems like such an exciting way to live my life.

15. Norman bought that old jalopy _____ <u>the purpose</u> _____ working on it until it is completely restored.

16. When the teacher caught her student cheating on the final examination, she was so angry that she <u>tore</u> the test paper _____.

17. Exhausted from work, Bridget and Howard couldn't wait to <u>get away</u> _____ the city for a weekend.

18. Nancy is flying east next week to <u>attend</u> _____ her mother, who injured her hip when she slipped on the ice.

19. After not having spoken for over twenty years, the Talbot brothers finally <u>got together</u> _____ each other last weekend.

20. Do you <u>take</u> _____ your mother or your father in personality?

21. Joanna called to <u>apologize</u> _____ standing me up last night. It seems that her car broke down and her cell phone wasn't working.

WEEK 15

1. Are you <u>acquainted</u> _____ Joe's friends from school?

2. Trying to <u>keep up</u> _____ a baby is absolutely exhausting.

3. It was cruel of Tony to <u>laugh</u> _____ the woman when she slipped and fell on her face.

4. Because we really care for and support each other, our class <u>laughed</u> _____ love at Julie when she giggled uncontrollably during her presentation.

5. I think that tiny, furry kittens are the <u>epitome</u> _____ cuteness.

6. How is a student supposed to <u>obtain</u> knowledge _____ this teacher when she doesn't know much about her subject matter?

7. Lettie's bed is <u>covered</u> _____ the most beautiful comforter that I have ever seen.

8. Can you <u>cover</u> _____ me at the meeting today? I have to make an emergency visit to the dentist.

9. How was it possible for Veronica to <u>run</u> _____ _____ gas? You'd think she would have checked her gas gauge before setting out on the trip.

10. Jason declared himself <u>independent</u> _____ his parents the minute he turned eighteen by immediately moving into his own apartment.

11. I wish my husband had <u>pointed</u> _____ that I had spinach trapped in my teeth before I had my picture taken.

12. General Adams just <u>retired</u> _____ the military after 40 years of service.

13. Are these directions <u>clear</u> _____ you? I'm lost.

14. Nancy made a generous contribution to the American Heart Association _____ <u>the name</u> _____ her uncle, Ed.

15. Although my alarm clock failed to go off this morning, I made it to the train station <u>just</u> _____ <u>time</u> to make my train.

16. This dress is much too expensive for my budget, but I simply have to <u>try</u> it _____.

17. Do you think it is <u>appropriate</u> _____ a ten-year-old girl to wear make-up?

18. While Suzie <u>teared</u> _____ watching "Titanic," I laughed my head off.

19. Merrie no longer has <u>faith</u> _____ Wayne and is, therefore, divorcing him.

20. <u>Look out</u> _____ holes in the sidewalk; my mother fell into one and broke her hip.

21. Are you going to <u>vote</u> _____ the incumbent senator or for his opponent?

WEEK 16

1. The book <u>East of Eden</u> had such a profound <u>effect</u> _____ Molly that she decided to become a writer.

2. I borrowed my mother-in-law's pearls and lost them _____ <u>accident</u>. How am I going to tell her?

3. Can you think of a good excuse to <u>get</u> Santiago _____ _____ his dreaded blind date?

4. Maria has <u>dreamed</u> _____ being a singer since she was a small child.

5. Be sure to <u>compliment</u> Scott _____ his new haircut. He's very sensitive about it.

6. No matter how hard she tries, Andrea finds it impossible to get along _____ her boss.

7. Come on over Friday night and we'll spend the evening eating, drinking, and gossiping _____ everyone at work.

8. No matter how hard I study, I never feel prepared _____ my math exams.

9. Help!!! The kitchen is _____ fire.

10. Martin Luther King lived his life fighting _____ racial equality.

11. This school never has an adequate supply _____ writing paper.

12. I think that each class should be supplied _____ enough paper to last a year.

13. When asked if he is only dating Nora, Henri answered, "_____ a way." What does that mean?

14. Are you positive _____ your answer because I think you're wrong.

15. Do you really think that one detergent is inferior _____ another, or do you think that they're all just about the same?

16. It's the dream of people around the world to be safe _____ violence.

17. Albert Einstein has long been thought _____ as one of the greatest minds in history.

18. I spent the entire night thinking _____ Miguel's marriage proposal, and I still don't know how to answer.

19. Are you going to recommend Dennis _____ the promotion?

20. I read a novel by Edith Wharton because my English teacher recommended her work _____ me.

21. Martha takes such delight _____ her grandchildren. It's fun to see.

WEEK 17

MONDAY

1. Emily's <u>solution</u> _____ the high cost of renting in New York City was to share a studio apartment with two other girls.

2. How do you like <u>working</u> _____ the new boss? Is he a slave-driver?

3. My grandmother always said that chocolate was <u>good</u> _____ colds.

4. I hate to <u>bring</u> _____ this painful issue, but did you remember to pay the Visa bill?

5. Samantha <u>put</u> _____ writing her term paper until the last possible moment.

6. I've always <u>preferred</u> coffee _____ tea. How about you?

7. Mr. Stein was infuriated when his dinner was <u>interrupted</u> _____ telephone solicitors.

TUESDAY

1. Emily's <u>solution</u> _____ the high cost of renting in New York City was to share a studio apartment with two other girls.

2. How do you like <u>working</u> _____ the new boss? Is he a slave-driver?

3. My grandmother always said that chocolate was <u>good</u> _____ colds.

4. I hate to <u>bring</u> _____ this painful issue, but did you remember to pay the Visa bill?

5. Samantha <u>put</u> _____ writing her term paper until the last possible moment.

6. I've always <u>preferred</u> coffee _____ tea. How about you?

7. Mr. Stein was infuriated when his dinner was <u>interrupted</u> _____ telephone solicitors.

8. Remind me to <u>check</u> _____ the weather forecast before we leave for the airport.

9. You'll have to ask Doug for permission to serve coffee in the classroom because he's _____ <u>charge</u> _____ school maintenance.

10. Jorge was kind to <u>drop</u> me _____ at work today since it took him out of his way.

11. Do you mind if I <u>look</u> _____ <u>with</u> you? I forgot my grammar book.

12. Can you believe that Barbara <u>took</u> money _____ her grandmother to buy a dress for the prom? Her grandmother can barely afford her rent.

13. Teenagers often <u>rebel</u> _____ the rules their parents set for them.

14. Do you have any <u>confidence</u> _____ the new manager? I don't.

WEDNESDAY

1. Emily's <u>solution</u> _____ the high cost of renting in New York City was to share a studio apartment with two other girls.

2. How do you like <u>working</u> _____ the new boss? Is he a slave-driver?

3. My grandmother always said that chocolate was <u>good</u> _____ colds.

4. I hate to <u>bring</u> _____ this painful issue, but did you remember to pay the Visa bill?

5. Samantha <u>put</u> _____ writing her term paper until the last possible moment.

6. I've always <u>preferred</u> coffee _____ tea. How about you?

7. Mr. Stein was infuriated when his dinner was <u>interrupted</u> _____ telephone solicitors.

8. Remind me to <u>check</u> _____ the weather forecast before we leave for the airport.

9. You'll have to ask Doug for permission to serve coffee in the classroom because he's _____ <u>charge</u> _____ school maintenance.

10. Jorge was kind to <u>drop</u> me _____ at work today since it took him out of his way.

11. Do you mind if I <u>look</u> _____ <u>with</u> you? I forgot my grammar book.

12. Can you believe that Barbara <u>took</u> money _____ her grand-mother to buy a dress for the prom? Her grandmother can barely afford her rent.

13. Teenagers often <u>rebel</u> _____ the rules their parents set for them.

14. Do you have any <u>confidence</u> _____ the new manager? I don't.

15. Come help me <u>pick</u> _____ a wedding present for Joe and Ann. I just don't know what to get them.

16. Daniel decided to move to Oregon _____ the <u>strength</u> _____ the job offer he received.

17. Don't forget to <u>call</u> _____ a dinner reservation early today. That restaurant gets booked quickly.

18. Mary can't wait to <u>get through</u> _____ April because it's the busiest time for an accountant.

19. John tried and tried to <u>get through</u> _____ his mother, but her phone was busy for four hours. Frustrated, he finally drove to her house to make sure she was okay.

20. Jim swears that not even once _____ <u>his life</u> has he told a lie.

21. Don't you think that too much make-up <u>detracts</u> _____ a woman's natural beauty?

THURSDAY

1. Emily's <u>solution</u> _____ the high cost of renting in New York City was to share a studio apartment with two other girls.

2. How do you like <u>working</u> _____ the new boss? Is he a slave-driver?

3. My grandmother always said that chocolate was <u>good</u> _____ colds.

4. I hate to <u>bring</u> _____ this painful issue, but did you remember to pay the Visa bill?

5. Samantha <u>put</u> _____ writing her term paper until the last possible moment.

6. I've always <u>preferred</u> coffee _____ tea. How about you?

7. Mr. Stein was infuriated when his dinner was <u>interrupted</u> _____ telephone solicitors.

8. Remind me to <u>check</u> _____ the weather forecast before we leave for the airport.

9. You'll have to ask Doug for permission to serve coffee in the classroom because he's _____ <u>charge</u> _____ school maintenance.

10. Jorge was kind to <u>drop</u> me _____ at work today since it took him out of his way.

11. Do you mind if I <u>look</u> _____ <u>with</u> you? I forgot my grammar book.

12. Can you believe that Barbara <u>took</u> money _____ her grand-mother to buy a dress for the prom? Her grandmother can barely afford her rent.

13. Teenagers often <u>rebel</u> _____ the rules their parents set for them.

14. Do you have any <u>confidence</u> _____ the new manager? I don't.

15. Come help me <u>pick</u> _____ a wedding present for Joe and Ann. I just don't know what to get them.

16. Daniel decided to move to Oregon _____ the <u>strength</u> _____ the job offer he received.

17. Don't forget to <u>call</u> _____ a dinner reservation early today. That restaurant gets booked quickly.

18. Mary can't wait to <u>get through</u> _____ April because it's the busiest time for an accountant.

19. John tried and tried to <u>get through</u> _____ his mother, but her phone was busy for four hours. Frustrated, he finally drove to her house to make sure she was okay.

20. Jim swears that not even once _____ <u>his life</u> has he told a lie.

21. Don't you think that too much make-up <u>detracts</u> _____ a woman's natural beauty?

FRIDAY

1. Emily's <u>solution</u> _____ the high cost of renting in New York City was to share a studio apartment with two other girls.

2. How do you like <u>working</u> _____ the new boss? Is he a slave-driver?

3. My grandmother always said that chocolate was <u>good</u> _____ colds.

4. I hate to <u>bring</u> _____ this painful issue, but did you remember to pay the Visa bill?

5. Samantha <u>put</u> _____ writing her term paper until the last possible moment.

6. I've always <u>preferred</u> coffee _____ tea. How about you?

7. Mr. Stein was infuriated when his dinner was <u>interrupted</u> _____ telephone solicitors.

8. Remind me to <u>check</u> _____ the weather forecast before we leave for the airport.

9. You'll have to ask Doug for permission to serve coffee in the classroom because he's _____ <u>charge</u> _____ school maintenance.

10. Jorge was kind to <u>drop</u> me _____ at work today since it took him out of his way.

11. Do you mind if I <u>look</u> _____ <u>with</u> you? I forgot my grammar book.

12. Can you believe that Barbara <u>took</u> money _____ her grandmother to buy a dress for the prom? Her grandmother can barely afford her rent.

13. Teenagers often <u>rebel</u> _____ the rules their parents set for them.

14. Do you have any <u>confidence</u> _____ the new manager? I don't.

15. Come help me <u>pick</u> _____ a wedding present for Joe and Ann. I just don't know what to get them.

16. Daniel decided to move to Oregon _____ the <u>strength</u> _____ the job offer he received.

17. Don't forget to <u>call</u> _____ a dinner reservation early today. That restaurant gets booked quickly.

18. Mary can't wait to <u>get through</u> _____ April because it's the busiest time for an accountant.

19. John tried and tried to <u>get through</u> _____ his mother, but her phone was busy for four hours. Frustrated, he finally drove to her house to make sure she was okay.

20. Jim swears that not even once _____ <u>his life</u> has he told a lie.

21. Don't you think that too much make-up <u>detracts</u> _____ a woman's natural beauty?

DISCUSSION

1. Do you like <u>working for</u> your boss? Is he a "slave-driver"?

2. Do you <u>prefer</u> classical music <u>to</u> rock and roll?

3. When you were young, did you ever <u>take</u> anything <u>from</u> a store? Did you get caught?

4. Do you <u>put off</u> chores and procrastinate, or do you "dive right in" and get to work immediately?

5. What part of your day can't you wait to <u>get through with</u>? What part of your day do you "savor" and really enjoy?

WEEK 18

MONDAY

1. The baseball game was postponed _____ account _____ rain.

2. Although Jose is a brilliant physicist, he has absolutely no <u>ability</u> _____ other scientific fields.

3. Sophie was <u>adamant</u> _____ her decision to drop out of high school. Nobody could reason with her, for her mind was made up.

4. John can't <u>depend</u> _____ his parents for college tuition because his father was recently laid off.

5. Roberto seems to <u>live</u> _____ a diet of potato chips and cola.

6. I'm so <u>excited</u> _____ my vacation this year: it's going to be my first time on an airplane.

TUESDAY

1. The baseball game was postponed _____ account _____ rain.

2. Although Jose is a brilliant physicist, he has absolutely no <u>ability</u> _____ other scientific fields.

3. Sophie was <u>adamant</u> _____ her decision to drop out of high school. Nobody could reason with her, for her mind was made up.

4. John can't <u>depend</u> _____ his parents for college tuition because his father was recently laid off.

5. Roberto seems to <u>live</u> _____ a diet of potato chips and cola.

6. I'm so <u>excited</u> _____ my vacation this year: it's going to be my first time on an airplane.

7. While I catch many colds, I seem to be <u>immune</u> _____ stomach viruses.

8. Are you <u>pleased</u> _____ your new job, or are you finding it to be too demanding?

9. It seems that the burglars <u>broke</u> _____ the house by first disabling the security system.

10. The telephone solicitor <u>asked</u> _____ donations for his charity.

11. Jan can't wait to <u>get done</u> _____ this project. He's been working on it for a month.

12. Were you <u>invited</u> _____ Lindsey's wedding? I wasn't and I'm really upset about it.

13. I <u>shuddered</u> _____ the gash on Catherine's cheek and had to turn away for fear of fainting.

14. It seems like a pain in the neck right now, but finishing your education will pay off _____ the <u>long run</u>.

WEDNESDAY

1. The baseball game was postponed _____ <u>account</u> _____ rain.

2. Although Jose is a brilliant physicist, he has absolutely no <u>ability</u> _____ other scientific fields.

3. Sophie was <u>adamant</u> _____ her decision to drop out of high school. Nobody could reason with her, for her mind was made up.

4. John can't <u>depend</u> _____ his parents for college tuition because his father was recently laid off.

5. Roberto seems to <u>live</u> _____ a diet of potato chips and cola.

6. I'm so <u>excited</u> _____ my vacation this year: it's going to be my first time on an airplane.

7. While I catch many colds, I seem to be <u>immune</u> _____ stomach viruses.

8. Are you <u>pleased</u> _____ your new job, or are you finding it to be too demanding?

9. It seems that the burglars <u>broke</u> _____ the house by first disabling the security system.

10. The telephone solicitor <u>asked</u> _____ donations for his charity.

11. Jan can't wait to <u>get</u> <u>done</u> _____ this project. He's been working on it for a month.

12. Were you <u>invited</u> _____ Lindsey's wedding? I wasn't and I'm really upset about it.

13. I <u>shuddered</u> _____ the gash on Catherine's cheek and had to turn away for fear of fainting.

14. It seems like a pain in the neck right now, but finishing your education will pay off_____ <u>the</u> <u>long</u> <u>run</u>.

15. It's difficult to imagine that Henry will stay at this job _____ <u>very</u> <u>long</u> since he already can't stand it.

16. Would someone call the custodian for Ms. Johnson. She can't get the television to <u>turn</u> _____.

17. Don't forget to <u>turn</u> _____ the fan when you leave so that electricity isn't wasted.

18. Joanna was so <u>thrilled</u> _____ the roller coaster that she rode it eleven times.

19. Because the elderly are so <u>vulnerable</u> _____ serious illness, they are always among the first to receive the flu shot.

20. How many Pesos are <u>equal</u> _____ $5.75?

21. Why can't Ben and Hal <u>cooperate</u> _____ each other instead of fighting all the time?

THURSDAY

1. The baseball game was postponed _____ <u>account</u> _____ rain.

2. Although Jose is a brilliant physicist, he has absolutely no <u>ability</u> _____ other scientific fields.

3. Sophie was <u>adamant</u> _____ her decision to drop out of high school. Nobody could reason with her, for her mind was made up.

4. John can't <u>depend</u> _____ his parents for college tuition because his father was recently laid off.

5. Roberto seems to <u>live</u> _____ a diet of potato chips and cola.

6. I'm so <u>excited</u> _____ my vacation this year: it's going to be my first time on an airplane.

7. While I catch many colds, I seem to be <u>immune</u> _____ stomach viruses.

8. Are you <u>pleased</u> _____ your new job, or are you finding it to be too demanding?

9. It seems that the burglars <u>broke</u> _____ the house by first disabling the security system.

10. The telephone solicitor <u>asked</u> _____ donations for his charity.

11. Jan can't wait to <u>get</u> <u>done</u> _____ this project. He's been working on it for a month.

12. Were you <u>invited</u> _____ Lindsey's wedding? I wasn't and I'm really upset about it.

13. I <u>shuddered</u> _____ the gash on Catherine's cheek and had to turn away for fear of fainting.

14. It seems like a pain in the neck right now, but finishing your education will pay off _____ the long run.

15. It's difficult to imagine that Henry will stay at this job _____ very long since he already can't stand it.

16. Would someone call the custodian for Ms. Johnson. She can't get the television to turn _____.

17. Don't forget to turn _____ the fan when you leave so that electricity isn't wasted.

18. Joanna was so thrilled _____ the roller coaster that she rode it eleven times.

19. Because the elderly are so vulnerable _____ serious illness, they are always among the first to receive the flu shot.

20. How many Pesos are equal _____ $5.75?

21. Why can't Ben and Hal cooperate _____ each other instead of fighting all the time?

FRIDAY

1. The baseball game was postponed _____ account _____ rain.

2. Although Jose is a brilliant physicist, he has absolutely no ability _____ other scientific fields.

3. Sophie was adamant _____ her decision to drop out of high school. Nobody could reason with her, for her mind was made.

4. John can't depend _____ his parents for college tuition because his father was recently laid off.

5. Roberto seems to live _____ a diet of potato chips and cola.

6. I'm so excited _____ my vacation this year: it's going to be my first time on an airplane.

7. While I catch many colds, I seem to be <u>immune</u> _____ stomach viruses.

8. Are you <u>pleased</u> _____ your new job, or are you finding it to be too demanding?

9. It seems that the burglars <u>broke</u> _____ the house by first disabling the security system.

10. The telephone solicitor <u>asked</u> _____ donations for his charity.

11. Jan can't wait to <u>get done</u> _____ this project. He's been working on it for a month.

12. Were you <u>invited</u> _____ Lindsey's wedding? I wasn't and I'm really upset about it.

13. I <u>shuddered</u> _____ the gash on Catherine's cheek and had to turn away for fear of fainting.

14. It seems like a pain in the neck right now, but finishing your education will pay off _____ <u>the long run</u>.

15. It's difficult to imagine that Henry will stay at this job _____ <u>very long</u> since he already can't stand it.

16. Would someone call the custodian for Ms. Johnson. She can't get the television to <u>turn</u> _____.

17. Don't forget to <u>turn</u> _____ the fan when you leave so that electricity isn't wasted.

18. Joanna was so <u>thrilled</u> _____ the roller coaster that she rode it eleven times.

19. Because the elderly are so <u>vulnerable</u> _____ serious illness, they are always among the first to receive the flu shot.

20. How many Pesos are <u>equal</u> _____ $5.75?

21. Why can't Ben and Hal <u>cooperate</u> _____ each other instead of fighting all the time?

DISCUSSION

1. Describe what you eat for breakfast each morning. Are you <u>living on</u> a healthy diet? How might you improve your diet? Name three changes you could make.

2. Will you remain in this city <u>for very long</u>? How long? Where do you think you will go when you leave here?

3. Name an upcoming event that you are really <u>excited about</u>.

4. Are you <u>pleased with</u> the progress that you are making in English? Why? Why not? What still really needs work?

5. What opinion are you <u>adamant about</u>? Can you imagine ever changing your feelings on this topic?

WEEK 19

MONDAY

1. It was generous of the teenagers to let the elderly man <u>go ahead</u> _____ them.

2. Texas is <u>rich</u> _____ oil.

3. Trust me. I'm only working on this project because the boss <u>forced</u> me _____ it.

4. Melanie's mother was so <u>proud</u> _____ her for graduating first in her class.

5. Mr. Lopez has a very odd <u>method</u> _____ teaching biology: he hands out the book the first day of class and tells you to read it and be ready for the final.

6. Did you <u>apply</u> _____ the sales job that just opened? I did.

7. If you decide you want to go to college next year, you must <u>apply</u> _____ each school by the end of January.

TUESDAY

1. It was generous of the teenagers to let the elderly man <u>go ahead</u> _____ them.

2. Texas is <u>rich</u> _____ oil.

3. Trust me. I'm only working on this project because the boss <u>forced</u> me _____ it.

4. Melanie's mother was so <u>proud</u> _____ her for graduating first in her class.

5. Mr. Lopez has a very odd <u>method</u> _____ teaching biology: he hands out the book the first day of class and tells you to read it and be ready for the final.

6. Did you <u>apply</u> _____ the sales job that just opened? I did.

7. If you decide you want to go to college next year, you must <u>apply</u> _____ each school by the end of January.

8. I love my dog! No matter how untrue my friends have been, he stays <u>loyal</u> _____ me.

9. <u>Prior</u> _____ my moving to San Diego, I lived in Boston.

10. <u>By</u> what <u>means</u> _____ transportation are you traveling to Los Angeles?

11. Debbie gets so nervous when she's in the <u>presence</u> _____ her math professor that she can't speak an intelligible word.

12. After Toby gained 20 pounds last summer, he couldn't <u>fit</u> _____ any of his clothes.

13. Don't <u>throw</u> _____ the empty soda bottles. Recycle them!

14. I will forever be <u>obligated</u> _____ my college roommate _____ tutoring me in Calculus.

WEDNESDAY

1. It was generous of the teenagers to let the elderly man <u>go ahead</u> _____ them.

2. Texas is <u>rich</u> _____ oil.

3. Trust me. I'm only working on this project because the boss <u>forced</u> me _____ it.

4. Melanie's mother was so <u>proud</u> _____ her for graduating first in her class.

5. Mr. Lopez has a very odd <u>method</u> _____ teaching biology: he hands out the book the first day of class and tells you to read it and be ready for the final.

6. Did you <u>apply</u> _____ the sales job that just opened? I did.

7. If you decide you want to go to college next year, you must <u>apply</u> _____ each school by the end of January.

8. I love my dog! No matter how untrue my friends have been, he stays <u>loyal</u> _____ me.

9. <u>Prior</u> _____ my moving to San Diego, I lived in Boston.

10. <u>By</u> what <u>means</u> _____ transportation are you traveling to Los Angeles?

11. Debbie gets so nervous when she's in the <u>presence</u> _____ her math professor that she can't speak an intelligible word.

12. After Toby gained 20 pounds last summer, he couldn't <u>fit</u> _____ any of his clothes.

13. Don't <u>throw</u> _____ the empty soda bottles. Recycle them!

14. I will forever be <u>obligated</u> _____ my college roommate _____ tutoring me in Calculus.

15. The professor assigned a paper _____ <u>lieu</u> _____ a final exam.

16. If you <u>come</u> _____ my journal, please don't read it. It's private.

17. Because she grew up in extreme poverty, Margarita is a strong <u>proponent</u> _____ all programs that support the poor.

18. When you visit Miyuko, <u>take</u> your shoes _____ before entering her house.

19. Just think, _____ <u>no time</u> <u>at</u> <u>all</u> you'll be fluent in English!

20. While I'm on vacation, my son is <u>checking</u> _____ _____ my elderly parents for me.

21. Why do you think Aunt Rita <u>disapproves</u> _____ Uncle Stan's job with such vehemence?

THURSDAY

1. It was generous of the teenagers to let the elderly man go ahead _____ them.

2. Texas is rich _____ oil.

3. Trust me. I'm only working on this project because the boss forced me _____ it.

4. Melanie's mother was so proud _____ her for graduating first in her class.

5. Mr. Lopez has a very odd method _____ teaching biology: he hands out the book the first day of class and tells you to read it and be ready for the final.

6. Did you apply _____ the sales job that just opened? I did.

7. If you decide you want to go to college next year, you must apply _____ each school by the end of January.

8. I love my dog! No matter how untrue my friends have been, he stays loyal _____ me.

9. Prior _____ my moving to San Diego, I lived in Boston.

10. By what means _____ transportation are you traveling to Los Angeles?

11. Debbie gets so nervous when she's in the presence _____ her math professor that she can't speak an intelligible word.

12. After Toby gained 20 pounds last summer, he couldn't fit _____ any of his clothes.

13. Don't throw _____ the empty soda bottles. Recycle them!

14. I will forever be obligated _____ my college roommate tutoring me in Calculus.

15. The professor assigned a paper _____ lieu _____ a final exam.

16. If you <u>come</u> _____ my journal, please don't read it. It's private.

17. Because she grew up in extreme poverty, Margarita is a strong <u>proponent</u> _____ all programs that support the poor..

18. When you visit Miyuko, <u>take</u> your shoes _____ before entering her house.

19. Just think, _____ <u>no time at all</u> you'll be fluent in English!

20. While I'm on vacation, my son is <u>checking</u> _____ _____ my elderly parents for me.

21. Why do you think Aunt Rita <u>disapproves</u> _____ Uncle Stan's job with such vehemence?

FRIDAY

1. It was generous of the teenagers to let the elderly man <u>go ahead</u> _____ them.

2. Texas is <u>rich</u> _____ oil.

3. Trust me. I'm only working on this project because the boss <u>forced</u> me _____ it.

4. Melanie's mother was so <u>proud</u> _____ her for graduating first in her class.

5. Mr. Lopez has a very odd <u>method</u> _____ teaching biology: he hands out the book the first day of class and tells you to read it and be ready for the final.

6. Did you <u>apply</u> _____ the sales job that just opened? I did.

7. If you decide you want to go to college next year, you must <u>apply</u> _____ each school by the end of January.

8. I love my dog! No matter how untrue my friends have been, he stays <u>loyal</u> _____ me.

9. <u>Prior</u> _____ my moving to San Diego, I lived in Boston.

10. <u>By</u> what <u>means</u> _____ transportation are you traveling to Los Angeles?

11. Debbie gets so nervous when she's in the <u>presence</u> _____ her math professor that she can't speak an intelligible word.

12. After Toby gained 20 pounds last summer, he couldn't <u>fit</u> _____ any of his clothes.

13. Don't <u>throw</u> _____ the empty soda bottles. Recycle them!

14. I will forever be <u>obligated</u> _____ my college roommate _____ tutoring me in Calculus.

15. The professor assigned a paper _____ <u>lieu</u> _____ a final exam.

16. If you <u>come</u> _____ my journal, please don't read it. It's private.

17. Because she grew up in extreme poverty, Margarita is a strong <u>proponent</u> _____ all programs that support the poor.

18. When you visit Miyuko, <u>take</u> your shoes _____ before entering her house.

19. Just think, _____ <u>no time</u> <u>at</u> <u>all</u> you'll be fluent in English!

20. While I'm on vacation, my son is <u>checking</u> _____ _____ my elderly parents for me.

21. Why do you think Aunt Rita <u>disapproves</u> _____ Uncle Stan's job with such vehemence?

DISCUSSION

1. Name something that you vehemently <u>disapprove of</u>.

2. Do people <u>take off</u> their shoes before entering your home? Is this usual behavior in your country?

3. Complete the following: When I am <u>(in)</u> the <u>presence</u> <u>of</u> _____, I get nervous and forget all of my English.

4. Name something that you've done in the last few years that you are very <u>proud of</u>.

5. <u>Prior to</u> moving to this city, where did you live? Which city do you like better?

WEEK 20

MONDAY

1. Sixteen ounces is <u>equivalent</u> _____ one pound.

2. Don't believe what Nancy says. She has a <u>tendency</u> _____ lie.

3. Whenever my mother-in-law comes to visit, she tries to <u>take</u> _____ my house by telling me how to cook, what to cook, and how to discipline my children.

4. For our twenty-fifth anniversary, let's go to a hotel that will <u>wait</u> _____ us hand and foot.

5. I'm running late. Will you still be able to <u>wait</u> _____ me?

6. I can't afford the <u>cost</u> _____ living alone. I'm going to have to get a roommate.

7. Were you as <u>disappointed</u> _____ the last James Bond movie as I was? It was dreadful.

TUESDAY

1. Sixteen ounces is <u>equivalent</u> _____ one pound.

2. Don't believe what Nancy says. She has a <u>tendency</u> _____ lie.

3. Whenever my mother-in-law comes to visit, she tries to <u>take</u> _____ my house by telling me how to cook, what to cook, and how to discipline my children.

4. For our twenty-fifth anniversary, let's go to a hotel that will <u>wait</u> _____ us hand and foot.

5. I'm running late. Will you still be able to <u>wait</u> _____ me?

6. I can't afford the <u>cost</u> _____ living alone. I'm going to have to get a roommate.

7. Were you as <u>disappointed</u> _____ the last James Bond movie as I was? It was dreadful.

8. The Smiths got divorced after thirty years of marriage _____ <u>the grounds</u> _____ incompatibility.

9. Has Max been _____ <u>contact</u> _____ you? I haven't heard from him in ages.

10. Brian is so <u>full</u> _____ himself. Don't you agree?

11. Todd and Lisa want to "tie the knot," but they are only fifteen, so they are going to need their parents' <u>consent</u> _____ marriage.

12. You won't have any trouble with English 205. _____ <u>many respects</u>, it's just an extension of English 101.

13. Is it really <u>necessary</u> _____ a student to edit his paper three times? My English teacher maintains that it is.

14. Carly has been sick with the flu for so long she's afraid she's never going to <u>recover</u> _____ it.

WEDNESDAY

1. Sixteen ounces is <u>equivalent</u> _____ one pound.

2. Don't believe what Nancy says. She has a <u>tendency</u> _____ lie.

3. Whenever my mother-in-law comes to visit, she tries to <u>take</u> _____ my house by telling me how to cook, what to cook, and how to discipline my children.

4. For our twenty-fifth anniversary, let's go to a hotel that will <u>wait</u> _____ us hand and foot.

5. I'm running late. Will you still be able to <u>wait</u> _____ me?

6. I can't afford the <u>cost</u> _____ living alone. I'm going to have to get a roommate.

7. Were you as <u>disappointed</u> _____ the last James Bond movie as I was? It was dreadful.

8. The Smiths got divorced after thirty years of marriage _____ <u>the grounds</u> _____ incompatibility.

9. Has Max been _____ <u>contact</u> _____ you? I haven't heard from him in ages.

10. Brian is so <u>full</u> _____ himself. Don't you agree?

11. Todd and Lisa want to "tie the knot," but they are only fifteen, so they are going to need their parents' <u>consent</u> _____ marriage.

12. You won't have any trouble with English 205. _____ <u>many respects</u>, it's just an extension of English 101.

13. Is it really <u>necessary</u> _____ a student to edit his paper three times? My English teacher maintains that it is.

14. Carly has been sick with the flu for so long she's afraid she's never going to <u>recover</u> _____ it.

15. Alberto Sanchez is the absolute <u>authority</u> _____ ancient Mayan crafts.

16. Remember to <u>pick</u> _____ marshmallows for the bonfire tonight. We want to make S'mores.

17. Why does Joseph have such <u>antipathy</u> _____ our new chemistry teacher? He seems like such a nice, capable professor.

18. Do you think that men or women are more <u>faithful</u> _____ their spouses?

19. How long has Charlotte been <u>married</u> _____ Martin? Is it possible that it's been 53 years?

20. Francois has been trying to speak to his boss for two weeks, but it's been impossible to gain <u>access</u> _____ him.

21. I'm forever <u>indebted</u> _____ my first grade teacher for teaching me how to read.

THURSDAY

1. Sixteen ounces is <u>equivalent</u> _____ one pound.

2. Don't believe what Nancy says. She has a <u>tendency</u> _____ lie.

3. Whenever my mother-in-law comes to visit, she tries to <u>take</u> _____ my house by telling me how to cook, what to cook, and how to discipline my children.

4. For our twenty-fifth anniversary, let's go to a hotel that will <u>wait</u> _____ us hand and foot.

5. I'm running late. Will you still be able to <u>wait</u> _____ me?

6. I can't afford the <u>cost</u> _____ living alone. I'm going to have to get a roommate.

7. Were you as <u>disappointed</u> _____ the last James Bond movie as I was? It was dreadful.

8. The Smiths got divorced after thirty years of marriage _____ <u>the grounds</u> _____ incompatibility.

9. Has Max been _____ <u>contact</u> _____ you? I haven't heard from him in ages.

10. Brian is so <u>full</u> _____ himself. Don't you agree?

11. Todd and Lisa want to "tie the knot," but they are only fifteen, so they are going to need their parents' <u>consent</u> _____ marriage.

12. You won't have any trouble with English 205. _____ <u>many respects</u>, it's just an extension of English 101.

13. Is it really <u>necessary</u> _____ a student to edit his paper three times? My English teacher maintains that it is.

14. Carly has been sick with the flu for so long she's afraid she's never going to <u>recover</u> _____ it.

15. Alberto Sanchez is the absolute <u>authority</u> _____ ancient Mayan crafts.

16. Remember to <u>pick</u> _____ marshmallows for the bonfire tonight. We want to make S'mores.

17. Why does Joseph have such <u>antipathy</u> _____ our new chemistry teacher? He seems like such a nice, capable professor.

18. Do you think that men or women are more <u>faithful</u> _____ their spouses?

19. How long has Charlotte been <u>married</u> _____ Martin? Is it possible that it's been 53 years?

20. Francois has been trying to speak to his boss for two weeks, but it's been impossible to gain <u>access</u> _____ him.

21. I'm forever <u>indebted</u> _____ my first grade teacher for teaching me how to read.

FRIDAY

1. Sixteen ounces is <u>equivalent</u> _____ one pound.

2. Don't believe what Nancy says. She has a <u>tendency</u> _____ lie.

3. Whenever my mother-in-law comes to visit, she tries to <u>take</u> _____ my house by telling me how to cook, what to cook, and how to discipline my children.

4. For our twenty-fifth anniversary, let's go to a hotel that will <u>wait</u> _____ us hand and foot.

5. I'm running late. Will you still be able to <u>wait</u> _____ me?

6. I can't afford the <u>cost</u> _____ living alone. I'm going to have to get a roommate.

7. Were you as <u>disappointed</u> _____ the last James Bond movie as I was? It was dreadful.

8. The Smiths got divorced after thirty years of marriage _____ <u>the</u> <u>grounds</u> _____ incompatibility.

9. Has Max been _____ <u>contact</u> _____ you? I haven't heard from him in ages.

10. Brian is so <u>full</u> _____ himself. Don't you agree?

11. Todd and Lisa want to "tie the knot," but they are only fifteen, so they are going to need their parents' <u>consent</u> _____ marriage.

12. You won't have any trouble with English 205. _____ <u>many respects</u>, it's just an extension of English 101.

13. Is it really <u>necessary</u> _____ a student to edit his paper three times? My English teacher maintains that it is.

14. Carly has been sick with the flu for so long she's afraid she's never going to <u>recover</u> _____ it.

15. Alberto Sanchez is the absolute <u>authority</u> _____ ancient Mayan crafts.

16. Remember to <u>pick</u> _____ marshmallows for the bonfire tonight. We want to make S'mores.

17. Why does Joseph have such <u>antipathy</u> _____ our new chemistry teacher? He seems like such a nice, capable professor.

18. Do you think that men or women are more <u>faithful</u> _____ their spouses?

19. How long has Charlotte been <u>married</u> _____ Martin? Is it possible that it's been 53 years?

20. Francois has been trying to speak to his boss for two weeks, but it's been impossible to gain <u>access</u> _____ him.

21. I'm forever <u>indebted</u> _____ my first grade teacher for teaching me how to read.

DISCUSSION

1. Do you have a <u>tendency to</u> be a "night owl" or an "early bird"?

2. What movie were you really <u>disappointed with</u>? Why?

3. Are you still <u>in contact with</u> any people from your childhood? How often do you communicate with them?

4. Name a famous person who you think is <u>full of</u> himself/herself.

5. Name a person whom you are <u>indebted to</u>. Describe him or her and tell what he/she did for you.

REVIEW WEEKS 17-20

WEEK 17

1. Emily's <u>solution</u> _____ the high cost of renting in New York City was to share a studio apartment with two other girls.

2. How do you like <u>working</u> _____ the new boss? Is he a slave-driver?

3. My grandmother always said that chocolate was <u>good</u> _____ colds.

4. I hate to <u>bring</u> _____ this painful issue, but did you remember to pay the Visa bill?

5. Samantha <u>put</u> _____ writing her term paper until the last possible moment.

6. I've always <u>preferred</u> coffee _____ tea. How about you?

7. Mr. Stein was infuriated when his dinner was <u>interrupted</u> _____ telephone solicitors.

8. Remind me to <u>check</u> _____ the weather forecast before we leave for the airport.

9. You'll have to ask Doug for permission to serve coffee in the classroom because he's _____ <u>charge</u> _____ school maintenance.

10. Jorge was kind to <u>drop</u> me _____ at work today since it took him out of his way.

11. Do you mind if I <u>look</u> _____ <u>with</u> you? I forgot my grammar book.

12. Can you believe that Barbara <u>took</u> money _____ her grandmother to buy a dress for the prom? Her grandmother can barely afford her rent.

13. Teenagers often <u>rebel</u> _____ the rules their parents set for them.

14. Do you have any <u>confidence</u> _____ the new manager? I don't.

15. Come help me <u>pick</u> _____ a wedding present for Joe and Ann. I just don't know what to get them.

16. Daniel decided to move to Oregon _____ the <u>strength</u> _____ the job offer he received.

17. Don't forget to <u>call</u> _____ a dinner reservation early today. That restaurant gets booked quickly.

18. Mary can't wait to <u>get through</u> _____ April because it's the busiest time for an accountant.

19. John tried and tried to <u>get through</u> _____ his mother, but her phone was busy for four hours. Frustrated, he finally drove to her house to make sure she was okay.

20. Jim swears that not even once _____ <u>his life</u> has he told a lie.

21. Don't you think that too much make-up <u>detracts</u> _____ a woman's natural beauty?

WEEK 18

1. The baseball game was postponed _____ <u>account</u> _____ rain.

2. Although Jose is a brilliant physicist, he has absolutely no <u>ability</u> _____ other scientific fields.

3. Sophie was <u>adamant</u> _____ her decision to drop out of high school. Nobody could reason with her, for her mind was made up.

4. John can't <u>depend</u> _____ his parents for college tuition because his father was recently laid off.

5. Roberto seems to <u>live</u> _____ a diet of potato chips and cola.

6. I'm so <u>excited</u> _____ my vacation this year: it's going to be my first time on an airplane.

7. While I catch many colds, I seem to be <u>immune</u> _____ stomach viruses.

8. Are you <u>pleased</u> _____ your new job, or are you finding it to be too demanding?

9. It seems that the burglars <u>broke</u> _____ the house by first disabling the security system.

10. The telephone solicitor <u>asked</u> _____ donations for his charity.

11. Jan can't wait to <u>get</u> <u>done</u> _____ this project. He's been working on it for a month.

12. Were you <u>invited</u> _____ Lindsey's wedding? I wasn't and I'm really upset about it.

13. I <u>shuddered</u> _____ the gash on Catherine's cheek and had to turn away for fear of fainting.

14. It seems like a pain in the neck right now, but finishing your education will pay off _____ <u>the</u> <u>long</u> <u>run</u>.

15. It's difficult to imagine that Henry will stay at this job _____ <u>very long</u> since he already can't stand it.

16. Would someone call the custodian for Ms. Johnson. She can't get the television to <u>turn</u> _____.

17. Don't forget to <u>turn</u> _____ the fan when you leave so that electricity isn't wasted.

18. Joanna was so <u>thrilled</u> _____ the roller coaster that she rode it eleven times.

19. Because the elderly are so <u>vulnerable</u> _____ serious illness, they are always among the first to receive the flu shot.

20. How many Pesos are <u>equal</u> _____ $5.75?

21. Why can't Ben and Hal <u>cooperate</u> _____ each other instead of fighting all the time?

WEEK 19

1. It was generous of the teenagers to let the elderly man <u>go ahead</u> _____ them.

2. Texas is <u>rich</u> _____ oil.

3. Trust me. I'm only working on this project because the boss <u>forced</u> me _____ it.

4. Melanie's mother was so <u>proud</u> _____ her for graduating first in her class.

5. Mr. Lopez has a very odd <u>method</u> _____ teaching biology: he hands out the book the first day of class and tells you to read it and be ready for the final.

6. Did you <u>apply</u> _____ the sales job that just opened? I did.

7. If you decide you want to go to college next year, you must <u>apply</u> _____ each school by the end of January.

8. I love my dog! No matter how untrue my friends have been, he stays <u>loyal</u> _____ me.

9. <u>Prior</u> _____ my moving to San Diego, I lived in Boston.

10. <u>By</u> what <u>means</u> _____ transportation are you traveling to Los Angeles?

11. Debbie gets so nervous when she's in the <u>presence</u> _____ her math professor that she can't speak an intelligible word.

12. After Toby gained 20 pounds last summer, he couldn't <u>fit</u> _____ any of his clothes.

13. Don't <u>throw</u> _____ the empty soda bottles. Recycle them!

14. I will forever be <u>obligated</u> _____ my college roommate _____ tutoring me in Calculus.

15. The professor assigned a paper _____ lieu _____ a final exam.

16. If you <u>come</u> _____ my journal, please don't read it. It's private.

17. Because she grew up in extreme poverty, Margarita is a strong <u>proponent</u> _____ all programs that support the poor.

18. When you visit Miyuko, <u>take</u> your shoes _____ before entering her house.

19. Just think, _____ <u>no time</u> <u>at</u> <u>all</u> you'll be fluent in English!

20. While I'm on vacation, my son is <u>checking</u> _____ _____ my elderly parents for me.

21. Why do you think Aunt Rita <u>disapproves</u> _____ Uncle Stan's job with such vehemence?

WEEK 20

1. Sixteen ounces is <u>equivalent</u> _____ one pound.

2. Don't believe what Nancy says. She has a <u>tendency</u> _____ lie.

3. Whenever my mother-in-law comes to visit, she tries to <u>take</u> _____ my house by telling me how to cook, what to cook, and how to discipline my children.

4. For our twenty-fifth anniversary, let's go to a hotel that will <u>wait</u> _____ us hand and foot.

5. I'm running late. Will you still be able to <u>wait</u> _____ me?

6. I can't afford the <u>cost</u> _____ living alone. I'm going to have to get a roommate.

7. Were you as <u>disappointed</u> _____ the last James Bond movie as I was? It was dreadful.

8. The Smiths got divorced after thirty years of marriage _____ <u>the</u> <u>grounds</u> _____ incompatibility.

9. Has Max been _____ contact _____ you? I haven't heard from him in ages.

10. Brian is so full _____ himself. Don't you agree?

11. Todd and Lisa want to "tie the knot," but they are only fifteen, so they are going to need their parents' consent _____ marriage.

12. You won't have any trouble with English 205. _____ many respects, it's just an extension of English 101.

13. Is it really necessary _____ a student to edit his paper three times? My English teacher maintains that it is.

14. Carly has been sick with the flu for so long she's afraid she's never going to recover _____ it.

15. Alberto Sanchez is the absolute authority _____ ancient Mayan crafts.

16. Remember to pick _____ marshmallows for the bonfire tonight. We want to make S'mores.

17. Why does Joseph have such antipathy _____ our new chemistry teacher? He seems like such a nice, capable professor.

18. Do you think that men or women are more faithful _____ their spouses?

19. How long has Charlotte been married _____ Martin? Is it possible that it's been 53 years?

20. Francois has been trying to speak to his boss for two weeks, but it's been impossible to gain access _____ him.

21. I'm forever indebted _____ my first grade teacher for teaching me how to read.

WEEK 21

MONDAY

1. I could never run a marathon; _____ best, I can only walk about three miles at a time.

2. I hope you don't mind my stopping in unannounced, but I was _____ the <u>vicinity</u> _____ your apartment and thought it might be fun to visit with you.

3. _____ the <u>circumstances</u>, Paul and Paulette have decided to postpone the gala.

4. When you run to the market, remember to buy milk. We're completely <u>out</u> _____ it.

5. When solicitors call during dinner, Uncle Charlie just <u>hangs</u> _____ _____ them.

6. John has complete <u>disdain</u> _____ anyone who tells lies.

7. Mr. Thompson humiliated that poor student _____ <u>front</u> _____ all of the other students.

TUESDAY

1. I could never run a marathon; _____ <u>best</u>, I can only walk about three miles at a time.

2. I hope you don't mind my stopping in unannounced, but I was _____ the <u>vicinity</u> _____ your apartment and thought it might be fun to visit with you.

3. _____ the <u>circumstances</u>, Paul and Paulette have decided to postpone the gala.

4. When you run to the market, remember to buy milk. We're completely <u>out</u> _____ it.

5. When solicitors call during dinner, Uncle Charlie just <u>hangs</u> _____ _____ them.

6. John has complete <u>disdain</u> _____ anyone who tells lies.

7. Mr. Thompson humiliated that poor student _____ <u>front</u> _____ all of the other students.

8. Biology 220 is _____ <u>far</u> the most difficult course that I have ever taken.

9. The newspaper made an <u>example</u> _____ the man who committed a hate crime.

10. I've often been <u>taken</u> _____ Tom Cruise. Do you see any similarities?

11. It would be nice to see Isabel <u>get</u> _____ the couch and turn off "the tube." She's been sitting there since she lost her job.

12. <u>As a consequence</u> _____ not putting any effort into her work, Peg was fired.

13. I'm so thirsty, but the vending machine is _____ _____ <u>order</u>.

14. Feel free to <u>drop</u> _____ _____ me whenever you're in the neighborhood.

WEDNESDAY

1. I could never run a marathon; _____ <u>best</u>, I can only walk about three miles at a time.

2. I hope you don't mind my stopping in unannounced, but I was _____ the <u>vicinity</u> _____ your apartment and thought it might be fun to visit with you.

3. _____ the circumstances, Paul and Paulette have decided to postpone the gala.

4. When you run to the market, remember to buy milk. We're completely out _____ it.

5. When solicitors call during dinner, Uncle Charlie just hangs _____ _____ them.

6. John has complete disdain _____ anyone who tells lies.

7. Mr. Thompson humiliated that poor student _____ front _____ all of the other students.

8. Biology 220 is _____ far the most difficult course that I have ever taken.

9. The newspaper made an example _____ the man who committed a hate crime.

10. I've often been taken _____ Tom Cruise. Do you see any similarities?

11. It would be nice to see Isabel get _____ the couch and turn off "the tube." She's been sitting there since she lost her job.

12. As a consequence _____ not putting any effort into her work, Peg was fired.

13. I'm so thirsty, but the vending machine is _____ _____ order.

14. Feel free to drop _____ _____ me whenever you're in the neighborhood.

15. That's not true. _____ the contrary, I'm in a fabulous mood!

16. It seems that the economy is falling _____ hard times.

17. A harvest holiday is common _____ many cultures.

18. Yet another basketball player has been accused _____ a violent crime. Why do you think the players are always getting into trouble?

19. The waiter just asked if this "Death By Chocolate" cake was satisfactory _____ me. Is he kidding?

20. Clayton said that his mother had the greatest <u>influence</u> _____ his life.

21. Cathy seems just a little too <u>attached</u> _____ her dog. She won't even go on vacation without him.

THURSDAY

1. I could never run a marathon; _____ <u>best</u>, I can only walk about three miles at a time.

2. I hope you don't mind my stopping in unannounced, but I was _____ the <u>vicinity</u> _____ your apartment and thought it might be fun to visit with you.

3. _____ the <u>circumstances</u>, Paul and Paulette have decided to postpone the gala.

4. When you run to the market, remember to buy milk. We're completely <u>out</u> _____ it.

5. When solicitors call during dinner, Uncle Charlie just <u>hangs</u> _____ _____ them.

6. John has complete <u>disdain</u> _____ anyone who tells lies.

7. Mr. Thompson humiliated that poor student _____ <u>front</u> _____ all of the other students.

8. Biology 220 is _____ <u>far</u> the most difficult course that I have ever taken.

9. The newspaper made an <u>example</u> _____ the man who committed a hate crime.

10. I've often been <u>taken</u> _____ Tom Cruise. Do you see any similarities?

11. It would be nice to see Isabel <u>get</u> _____ the couch and turn off "the tube." She's been sitting there since she lost her job.

12. <u>As a consequence</u> _____ not putting any effort into her work, Peg was fired.

13. I'm so thirsty, but the vending machine is _____ _____ <u>order</u>.

14. Feel free to <u>drop</u> _____ _____ me whenever you're in the neighborhood.

15. That's not true. _____ the <u>contrary</u>, I'm in a fabulous mood!

16. It seems that the economy is <u>falling</u> _____ hard times.

17. A harvest holiday is <u>common</u> _____ many cultures.

18. Yet another basketball player has been <u>accused</u> _____ a violent crime. Why do you think the players are always getting into trouble?

19. The waiter just asked if this "Death By Chocolate" cake was <u>satisfactory</u> _____ me. Is he kidding?

20. Clayton said that his mother had the greatest <u>influence</u> _____ his life.

21. Cathy seems just a little too <u>attached</u> _____ her dog. She won't even go on vacation without him.

FRIDAY

1. I could never run a marathon; _____ <u>best</u>, I can only walk about three miles at a time.

2. I hope you don't mind my stopping in unannounced, but I was _____ the <u>vicinity</u> _____ your apartment and thought it might be fun to visit with you.

3. _____ the <u>circumstances</u>, Paul and Paulette have decided to postpone the gala.

4. When you run to the market, remember to buy milk. We're completely <u>out</u> _____ it.

5. When solicitors call during dinner, Uncle Charlie just <u>hangs</u> _____ _____ them.

6. John has complete <u>disdain</u> _____ anyone who tells lies.

7. Mr. Thompson humiliated that poor student _____ <u>front</u> _____ all of the other students.

8. Biology 220 is _____ <u>far</u> the most difficult course that I have ever taken.

9. The newspaper made an <u>example</u> _____ the man who committed a hate crime.

10. I've often been <u>taken</u> _____ Tom Cruise. Do you see any similarities?

11. It would be nice to see Isabel <u>get</u> _____ the couch and turn off "the tube." She's been sitting there since she lost her job.

12. <u>As a consequence</u> _____ not putting any effort into her work, Peg was fired.

13. I'm so thirsty, but the vending machine is _____ _____ <u>order</u>.

14. Feel free to <u>drop</u> _____ _____ me whenever you're in the neighborhood.

15. That's not true. _____ the <u>contrary</u>, I'm in a fabulous mood!

16. It seems that the economy is <u>falling</u> _____ hard times.

17. A harvest holiday is <u>common</u> _____ many cultures.

18. Yet another basketball player has been <u>accused</u> _____ a violent crime. Why do you think the players are always getting into trouble?

19. The waiter just asked if this "Death By Chocolate" cake was <u>satisfactory</u> _____ me. Is he kidding?

20. Clayton said that his mother had the greatest <u>influence</u> _____ his life.

21. Cathy seems just a little too <u>attached</u> _____ her dog. She won't even go on vacation without him.

DISCUSSION

1. What is <u>by far</u> the most difficult thing you have ever had to learn?

2. Have you ever been <u>taken for</u> anyone famous? Who?

3. Do you like it when people <u>drop in on</u> you unannounced, or do you prefer that they call first? What is the custom in your country?

4. Are you a "couch potato"? When the weekend comes, is it difficult for you to <u>get off</u> the couch, or are you "out and about," busy and active?

5. Do you think that the economy is <u>falling on</u> hard times, or is it robust and thriving?

WEEK 22

MONDAY

1. Do you think that the death penalty <u>prevents</u> people _____ murdering others?

2. The young employee said that, _____ <u>course</u>, he'd stay late to finish the project.

3. I became a wedding planner completely _____ <u>chance</u> when nobody else was available to organize my baby sister's wedding.

4. The Oscar winner said he was forever <u>grateful</u> _____ the director of the movie.

5. The Olympic athlete was <u>grateful</u> _____ the chance to compete.

6. Mr. Peterson hasn't <u>communicated</u> _____ his siblings in over twenty years.

7. Let's pour lots of water on the campfire so that we make sure we really <u>put</u> it _____.

TUESDAY

1. Do you think that the death penalty <u>prevents</u> people _____ murdering others?

2. The young employee said that, _____ <u>course</u>, he'd stay late to finish the project.

3. I became a wedding planner completely _____ <u>chance</u> when nobody else was available to organize my baby sister's wedding.

4. The Oscar winner said he was forever <u>grateful</u> _____ the director of the movie.

5. The Olympic athlete was <u>grateful</u> _____ the chance to compete.

6. Mr. Peterson hasn't <u>communicated</u> _____ his siblings in over twenty years.

7. Let's pour lots of water on the campfire so that we make sure we really <u>put</u> it _____.

8. Leroy thought that the project would take at least three months to finish, but he completed it <u>ahead</u> _____ schedule.

9. Paula <u>dropped</u> _____ _____ college with just one semester to go!

10. I think I left my red sweater at your house. If you <u>stumble</u> _____ it, would you bring it to work tomorrow?

11. Ali knows that he can always <u>count</u> _____ his family to support him in times of crisis.

12. Sy <u>threw</u> _____ his hands in frustration when he couldn't balance his checkbook.

13. Do you think that the department store will <u>take</u> _____ this blouse? It tore to shreds in the washing machine.

14. The rowdy, inebriated students were <u>removed</u> _____ the auditorium when they started heckling the speaker.

WEDNESDAY

1. Do you think that the death penalty <u>prevents</u> people _____ murdering others?

2. The young employee said that, _____ <u>course</u>, he'd stay late to finish the project.

3. I became a wedding planner completely _____ <u>chance</u> when nobody else was available to organize my baby sister's wedding.

4. The Oscar winner said he was forever <u>grateful</u> _____ the director of the movie.

5. The Olympic athlete was <u>grateful</u> _____ the chance to compete.

6. Mr. Peterson hasn't <u>communicated</u> _____ his siblings in over twenty years.

7. Let's pour lots of water on the campfire so that we make sure we really <u>put</u> it _____.

8. Leroy thought that the project would take at least three months to finish, but he completed it <u>ahead</u> _____ schedule.

9. Paula <u>dropped</u> _____ _____ college with just one semester to go!

10. I think I left my red sweater at your house. If you <u>stumble</u> _____ it, would you bring it to work tomorrow?

11. Ali knows that he can always <u>count</u> _____ his family to support him in times of crisis.

12. Sy <u>threw</u> _____ his hands in frustration when he couldn't balance his checkbook.

13. Do you think that the department store will <u>take</u> _____ this blouse? It tore to shreds in the washing machine.

14. The rowdy, inebriated students were <u>removed</u> _____ the auditorium when they started heckling the speaker.

15. After a lovely nap, Simon decided it was time to <u>get back</u> _____ work.

16. _____ <u>day</u>, Superman is the mild mannered Clark Kent.

17. <u>Aside</u> _____ the bibliography, Jan has completely finished his term paper.

18. What factors do you think <u>lead</u> _____ Americans being so obese?

19. The junk drawer in my kitchen is filled with things that are <u>useful</u> _____ absolutely nothing.

20. May I have this old milk crate? While it's not <u>useful</u> _____ you, I think I can turn it into a funky coffee table.

21. <u>Hang</u> _____ your hats. The wind is really howling!

THURSDAY

1. Do you think that the death penalty <u>prevents</u> people _____ murdering others?

2. The young employee said that, _____ <u>course</u>, he'd stay late to finish the project.

3. I became a wedding planner completely _____ <u>chance</u> when nobody else was available to organize my baby sister's wedding.

4. The Oscar winner said he was forever <u>grateful</u> _____ the director of the movie.

5. The Olympic athlete was <u>grateful</u> _____ the chance to compete.

6. Mr. Peterson hasn't <u>communicated</u> _____ his siblings in over twenty years.

7. Let's pour lots of water on the campfire so that we make sure we really <u>put</u> it _____.

8. Leroy thought that the project would take at least three months to finish, but he completed it <u>ahead</u> _____ schedule.

9. Paula <u>dropped</u> _____ _____ college with just one semester to go!

10. I think I left my red sweater at your house. If you <u>stumble</u> _____ it, would you bring it to work tomorrow?

11. Ali knows that he can always <u>count</u> _____ his family to support him in times of crisis.

12. Sy <u>threw</u> _____ his hands in frustration when he couldn't balance his checkbook.

13. Do you think that the department store will <u>take</u> _____ this blouse? It tore to shreds in the washing machine.

14. The rowdy, inebriated students were <u>removed</u> _____ the auditorium when they started heckling the speaker.

15. After a lovely nap, Simon decided it was time to <u>get</u> <u>back</u> _____ work.

16. _____ <u>day</u>, Superman is the mild mannered Clark Kent.

17. <u>Aside</u> _____ the bibliography, Jan has completely finished his term paper.

18. What factors do you think <u>lead</u> _____ Americans being so obese?

19. The junk drawer in my kitchen is filled with things that are <u>useful</u> _____ absolutely nothing.

20. May I have this old milk crate? While it's not <u>useful</u> _____ you, I think I can turn it into a funky coffee table.

21. <u>Hang</u> _____ your hats. The wind is really howling!

FRIDAY

1. Do you think that the death penalty <u>prevents</u> people _____ murdering others?

2. The young employee said that, _____ <u>course</u>, he'd stay late to finish the project.

3. I became a wedding planner completely _____ <u>chance</u> when nobody else was available to organize my baby sister's wedding.

4. The Oscar winner said he was forever <u>grateful</u> _____ the director of the movie.

5. The Olympic athlete was <u>grateful</u> _____ the chance to compete.

6. Mr. Peterson hasn't <u>communicated</u> _____ his siblings in over twenty years.

7. Let's pour lots of water on the campfire so that we make sure we really <u>put</u> it _____.

8. Leroy thought that the project would take at least three months to finish, but he completed it <u>ahead</u> _____ schedule.

9. Paula <u>dropped</u> _____ _____ college with just one semester to go!

10. I think I left my red sweater at your house. If you <u>stumble</u> _____ it, would you bring it to work tomorrow?

11. Ali knows that he can always <u>count</u> _____ his family to support him in times of crisis.

12. Sy <u>threw</u> _____ his hands in frustration when he couldn't balance his checkbook.

13. Do you think that the department store will <u>take</u> _____ this blouse? It tore to shreds in the washing machine.

14. The rowdy, inebriated students were <u>removed</u> _____ the auditorium when they started heckling the speaker.

15. After a lovely nap, Simon decided it was time to <u>get</u> <u>back</u> _____ work.

16. _____ <u>day</u>, Superman is the mild mannered Clark Kent.

17. <u>Aside</u> _____ the bibliography, Jan has completely finished his term paper.

18. What factors do you think <u>lead</u> _____ Americans being so obese?

19. The junk drawer in my kitchen is filled with things that are <u>useful</u> _____ absolutely nothing.

20. May I have this old milk crate? While it's not <u>useful</u> _____ you, I think I can turn it into a funky coffee table.

21. <u>Hang</u> _____ your hats. The wind is really howling!

DISCUSSION

1. How often do you <u>communicate with</u> your siblings? How many siblings do you have?

2. Name three things that you are truly <u>grateful for</u>.

3. Who can you <u>count on</u> to be there for you when the "going gets tough"?

4. <u>Aside from</u> this class, of course, what's the best class you've ever taken? What made the class so exceptional?

5. What factors do you think <u>lead to</u> the obesity of Americans?

WEEK 23

MONDAY

1. The elderly woman <u>leaned</u> _____ her son as she walked into the church.

2. When I bake, I use apple sauce _____ <u>place</u> _____ oil so that my muffins and cookies have less fat.

3. I invited Mr. and Mrs. Morelli, <u>along</u> _____ their children, to our Christmas party.

4. _____ <u>theory</u>, the TV should work once I plug in this wire.

5. Elizabeth Taylor has been <u>divorced</u> _____ at least seven husbands.

6. When you land in Athens, be sure to <u>get</u> _____ <u>touch</u> _____ my family. They'll roll out the red carpet for you.

7. I wish my grandfather would drive a little faster. _____ <u>this rate</u>, we won't get to the movie until it's already started.

TUESDAY

1. The elderly woman <u>leaned</u> _____ her son as she walked into the church.

2. When I bake, I use apple sauce _____ <u>place</u> _____ oil so that my muffins and cookies have less fat.

3. I invited Mr. And Mrs. Morelli, <u>along</u> _____ their children, to our Christmas party.

4. _____ <u>theory</u>, the TV should work once I plug in this wire.

5. Elizabeth Taylor has been <u>divorced</u> _____ at least seven husbands.

6. When you land in Athens, be sure to <u>get</u> _____ <u>touch</u> _____ my family. They'll roll out the red carpet for you.

7. I wish my grandfather would drive a little faster. _____ <u>this rate</u>, we won't get to the movie until it's already started.

8. Do you think that Americans are <u>friendly</u> _____ foreigners?

9. Whatever <u>became</u> _____ Eduardo? He just disappeared from our lives.

10. Did Kelly really <u>ask</u> Alain _____ on a date? What did he say?

11. The teacher bellowed, "Please <u>desist</u> _____ talking in class!"

12. _____ <u>the one hand</u>, Friday evening sounds like the perfect time to get together to work on our final project.

13. _____ <u>the other hand</u>, though, who wants to work on Friday night?

14. After a nasty fight with my sister, I <u>went</u> _____ <u>a walk</u> to cool down.

WEDNESDAY

1. The elderly woman <u>leaned</u> _____ her son as she walked into the church.

2. When I bake, I use apple sauce _____ <u>place</u> _____ oil so that my muffins and cookies have less fat.

3. I invited Mr. and Mrs. Morelli, <u>along</u> _____ their children, to our Christmas party.

4. _____ <u>theory</u>, the TV should work once I plug in this wire.

5. Elizabeth Taylor has been <u>divorced</u> _____ at least seven husbands.

6. When you land in Athens, be sure to <u>get</u> _____ <u>touch</u> _____ my family. They'll roll out the red carpet for you.

7. I wish my grandfather would drive a little faster. _____ <u>this</u> <u>rate</u>, we won't get to the movie until it's already started.

8. Do you think that Americans are <u>friendly</u> _____ foreigners?

9. Whatever <u>became</u> _____ Eduardo? He just disappeared from our lives.

10. Did Kelly really <u>ask</u> Alain _____ on a date? What did he say?

11. The teacher bellowed, "Please <u>desist</u> _____ talking in class!"

12. _____ <u>the</u> <u>one</u> <u>hand</u>, Friday evening sounds like the perfect time to get together to work on our final project.

13. _____ <u>the</u> <u>other</u> <u>hand</u>, though, who wants to work on Friday night?

14. After a nasty fight with my sister, I <u>went</u> _____ <u>a</u> <u>walk</u> to cool down.

15. Maria hated living so far <u>away</u> _____ her family. She suffered from terrible homesickness.

16. This class didn't seem hard _____ <u>the</u> <u>beginning</u>, but now it's a killer.

17. The constant parties that my roommates give are a <u>hindrance</u> _____ my studying.

18. Lettie is so <u>critical</u> _____ her mother's cooking. Her mom should just refuse to cook anymore!

19. _____ <u>the</u> <u>whole</u>, this internship has been the best job experience I've ever had.

20. Due to budget cuts, the program is _____ <u>danger</u> _____being closed.

21. Roberto forgot to <u>call</u> _____ when he took a mental health day from work. As a result, he got fired.

THURSDAY

1. The elderly woman <u>leaned</u> _____ her son as she walked into the church.

2. When I bake, I use apple sauce _____ <u>place</u> _____ oil so that my muffins and cookies have less fat.

3. I invited Mr. and Mrs. Morelli, <u>along</u> _____ their children, to our Christmas party.

4. _____ <u>theory</u>, the TV should work once I plug in this wire.

5. Elizabeth Taylor has been <u>divorced</u> _____ at least seven husbands.

6. When you land in Athens, be sure to <u>get</u> _____ <u>touch</u> _____ my family. They'll roll out the red carpet for you.

7. I wish my grandfather would drive a little faster. _____ <u>this rate</u>, we won't get to the movie until it's already started.

8. Do you think that Americans are <u>friendly</u> _____ foreigners?

9. Whatever <u>became</u> _____ Eduardo? He just disappeared from our lives.

10. Did Kelly really <u>ask</u> Alain _____ on a date? What did he say?

11. The teacher bellowed, "Please <u>desist</u> _____ talking in class!"

12. _____ <u>the</u> <u>one</u> <u>hand</u>, Friday evening sounds like the perfect time to get together to work on our final project.

13. _____ <u>the</u> <u>other</u> <u>hand</u>, though, who wants to work on Friday night?

14. After a nasty fight with my sister, I <u>went</u> _____ <u>a walk</u> to cool down.

WEEK 23

15. Maria hated living so far <u>away</u> _____ her family. She suffered from terrible homesickness.

16. This class didn't seem hard _____ <u>the</u> <u>beginning</u>, but now it's a killer.

17. The constant parties that my roommates give are a <u>hindrance</u> _____ my studying.

18. Lettie is so <u>critical</u> _____ her mother's cooking. Her mom should just refuse to cook anymore!

19. _____ <u>the</u> <u>whole</u>, this internship has been the best job experience I've ever had.

20. Due to budget cuts, the program is _____ <u>danger</u> _____ being closed.

21. Roberto forgot to <u>call</u> _____ when he took a mental health day from work. As a result, he got fired.

FRIDAY

1. The elderly woman <u>leaned</u> _____ her son as she walked into the church.

2. When I bake, I use apple sauce _____ <u>place</u> _____ oil so that my muffins and cookies have less fat.

3. I invited Mr. and Mrs. Morelli, <u>along</u> _____ their children, to our Christmas party.

4. _____ <u>theory</u>, the TV should work once I plug in this wire.

5. Elizabeth Taylor has been <u>divorced</u> _____ at least seven husbands.

6. When you land in Athens, be sure to <u>get</u> _____ <u>touch</u> _____ my family. They'll roll out the red carpet for you.

7. I wish my grandfather would drive a little faster. _____ <u>this</u> <u>rate</u>, we won't get to the movie until it's already started.

8. Do you think that Americans are <u>friendly</u> _____ foreigners?

9. Whatever <u>became</u> _____ Eduardo? He just disappeared from our lives.

10. Did Kelly really <u>ask</u> Alain _____ on a date? What did he say?

11. The teacher bellowed, "Please <u>desist</u> _____ talking in class!"

12. _____ the <u>one hand</u>, Friday evening sounds like the perfect time to get together to work on our final project.

13. _____ the <u>other hand</u>, though, who wants to work on Friday night?

14. After a nasty fight with my sister, I <u>went</u> _____ <u>a walk</u> to cool down.

15. Maria hated living so far <u>away</u> _____ her family. She suffered from terrible homesickness.

16. This class didn't seem hard _____ <u>the beginning</u>, but now it's a killer.

17. The constant parties that my roommates give are a <u>hindrance</u> _____ my studying.

18. Lettie is so <u>critical</u> _____ her mother's cooking. Her mom should just refuse to cook anymore!

19. _____ the <u>whole</u>, this internship has been the best job experience I've ever had.

20. Due to budget cuts, the program is _____ <u>danger</u> _____ being closed.

21. Roberto forgot to <u>call</u> _____ when he took a mental health day from work. As a result, he got fired.

DISCUSSION

1. Are you generally <u>critical of</u> or <u>accepting of</u> your government's domestic policies? Your government's foreign policies? The United States' government's foreign policies?

2. <u>On the whole</u>, what's the best thing about living in this city? The worst?

3. What is your number one goal for this year? Name a <u>hindrance to</u> your completing that goal.

4. If you could <u>ask</u> one famous person <u>out</u> on a date, whom would you ask? Why? Where would you go?

5. Where is your favorite place to <u>go for a walk</u>?

WEEK 24

MONDAY

1. Luis tries to <u>get</u> <u>along</u> _____ his cousin Marco, but they just rub each other the wrong way.

2. Did you hear the news? Todd <u>got</u> <u>engaged</u> _____ a girl he met just two weeks ago!

3. Don't interrupt Brian right now. He's very <u>engaged</u> _____ his project.

4. Judy always has to be the center of attention. She'll do just about anything to <u>call</u> <u>attention</u> _____ herself.

5. Do you have any <u>knowledge</u> _____ Victorian literature? I have to write an essay and I really need help.

6. Pablo is trying his first case in court tomorrow, and he is so <u>anxious</u> _____it that he hasn't slept all week.

7. Look at the sculpture! It's <u>made</u> entirely _____ recycled trash.

TUESDAY

1. Luis tries to <u>get</u> <u>along</u> _____ his cousin Marco, but they just rub each other the wrong way.

2. Did you hear the news? Todd <u>got</u> <u>engaged</u> _____ a girl he met just two weeks ago!

3. Don't interrupt Brian right now. He's very <u>engaged</u> _____ his project.

4. Judy always has to be the center of attention. She'll do just about anything to <u>call</u> <u>attention</u> _____ herself.

5. Do you have any <u>knowledge</u> _____ Victorian literature? I have to write an essay and I really need help.

6. Pablo is trying his first case in court tomorrow, and he so <u>anxious</u> _____ it that he hasn't slept all week.

7. Look at the sculpture! It's <u>made</u> entirely _____ recycled trash.

8. _____ <u>order</u> _____ achieve his dream of becoming a professional basketball player, Emmet had to practice four hours every day.

9. Joy should never wear shocking pink lipstick. It's really not <u>becoming</u> _____ her.

10. _____ <u>the end</u> _____ <u>the day</u>, Tina is too worn out to do anything but come home, put on her p.j.'s, and watch TV.

11. Joe's boss likes him because he <u>puts</u> _____ a lot of overtime.

12. _____ <u>the moment</u>, Gustavo is too busy to take on any more clients.

13. Let's get to work on this baking and <u>dispense</u> _____ it as soon as possible so that we can head to the beach.

14. I wish that Benjamin would <u>refrain</u> _____ talking in class; he's driving me crazy!

WEDNESDAY

1. Luis tries to <u>get along</u> _____ his cousin Marco, but they just rub each other the wrong way.

2. Did you hear the news? Todd <u>got engaged</u> _____ a girl he met just two weeks ago!

3. Don't interrupt Brian right now. He's very <u>engaged</u> _____ his project.

4. Judy always has to be the center of attention. She'll do just about anything to <u>call attention</u> _____ herself.

5. Do you have any <u>knowledge</u> _____ Victorian literature? I have to write an essay and I really need help.

6. Pablo is trying his first case in court tomorrow, and he so <u>anxious</u> _____ it that he hasn't slept all week.

7. Look at the sculpture! It's <u>made</u> entirely _____ recycled trash.

8. _____ <u>order</u> _____ achieve his dream of becoming a professional basketball player, Emmet had to practice four hours every day.

9. Joy should never wear shocking pink lipstick. It's really not <u>becoming</u> _____ her.

10. _____ <u>the end</u> _____ <u>the day</u>, Tina is too worn out to do anything but come home, put on her p.j.'s, and watch TV.

11. Joe's boss likes him because he <u>puts</u> _____ a lot of overtime.

12. _____ <u>the moment</u>, Gustavo is too busy to take on any more clients.

13. Let's get to work on this baking and <u>dispense</u> _____ it as soon as possible so that we can head to the beach.

14. I wish that Benjamin would <u>refrain</u> _____ talking in class; he's driving me crazy!

15. When you <u>get back</u> _____ vacation, let's get together to discuss the new semester.

16. Look at that frightened little boy. He's <u>clinging</u> _____ his mother.

17. Unless Fabio <u>apologizes</u> _____ Gabbie, I don't think she'll ever talk to him again.

18. Danielle can't sing a note, but she's amazingly <u>good</u> _____ playing the piano.

19. Grandma always lived by one principle: be <u>good</u> _____ those you love.

20. Mauricio <u>gets</u> such a <u>kick</u> _____ _____ his little nephew.

21. With our family budget as tight as it is, going on vacation this year is _____ _____ the <u>question</u>.

THURSDAY

1. Luis tries to <u>get along</u> _____ his cousin Marco, but they just rub each other the wrong way.

2. Did you hear the news? Todd <u>got engaged</u> _____ a girl he met just two weeks ago!

3. Don't interrupt Brian right now. He's very <u>engaged</u> _____ his project.

4. Judy always has to be the center of attention. She'll do just about anything to <u>call attention</u> _____ herself.

5. Do you have any <u>knowledge</u> _____ Victorian literature? I have to write an essay and I really need help.

6. Pablo is trying his first case in court tomorrow, and he so <u>anxious</u> _____ it that he hasn't slept all week.

7. Look at the sculpture! It's <u>made</u> entirely _____ recycled trash.

8. _____ <u>order</u> _____ achieve his dream of becoming a professional basketball player, Emmet had to practice four hours every day.

9. Joy should never wear shocking pink lipstick. It's really not <u>becoming</u> _____ her.

10. _____ <u>the end</u> _____ <u>the day</u>, Tina is too worn out to do anything but come home, put on her p.j.'s, and watch TV.

11. Joe's boss likes him because he <u>puts</u> _____ a lot of overtime.

12. _____ the moment, Gustavo is too busy to take on any more clients.

13. Let's get to work on this baking and dispense _____ it as soon as possible so that we can head to the beach.

14. I wish that Benjamin would refrain _____ talking in class; he's driving me crazy!

15. When you get back _____ vacation, let's get together to discuss the new semester.

16. Look at that frightened little boy. He's clinging _____ his mother.

17. Unless Fabio apologizes _____ Gabbie, I don't think she'll ever talk to him again.

18. Danielle can't sing a note, but she's amazingly good _____ playing the piano.

19. Grandma always lived by one principle: be good _____ those you love.

20. Mauricio gets such a kick _____ _____ his little nephew.

21. With our family budget as tight as it is, going on vacation this year is _____ _____ the question.

FRIDAY

1. Luis tries to get along _____ his cousin Marco, but they just rub each other the wrong way.

2. Did you hear the news? Todd got engaged _____ a girl he met just two weeks ago!

3. Don't interrupt Brian right now. He's very engaged _____ his project.

4. Judy always has to be the center of attention. She'll do just about anything to call attention _____ herself.

5. Do you have any <u>knowledge</u> _____ Victorian literature? I have to write an essay and I really need help.

6. Pablo is trying his first case in court tomorrow, and he so <u>anxious</u> _____ it that he hasn't slept all week.

7. Look at the sculpture! It's <u>made</u> entirely _____ recycled trash.

8. _____ <u>order</u> _____ achieve his dream of becoming a professional basketball player, Emmet had to practice four hours every day.

9. Joy should never wear shocking pink lipstick. It's really not <u>becom-ing</u> _____ her.

10. _____ <u>the end</u> _____ <u>the day</u>, Tina is too worn out to do anything but come home, put on her p.j.'s, and watch TV.

11. Joe's boss likes him because he <u>puts</u> _____ a lot of overtime.

12. _____ <u>the moment</u>, Gustavo is too busy to take on any more clients.

13. Let's get to work on this baking and <u>dispense</u> _____ it as soon as possible so that we can head to the beach.

14. I wish that Benjamin would <u>refrain</u> _____ talking in class; he's driving me crazy!

15. When you <u>get back</u> _____ vacation, let's get together to discuss the new semester.

16. Look at that frightened little boy. He's <u>clinging</u> _____ his mother.

17. Unless Fabio <u>apologizes</u> _____ Gabbie, I don't think she'll ever talk to him again.

18. Danielle can't sing a note, but she's amazingly <u>good</u> _____ play-ing the piano.

19. Grandma always lived by one principle: be <u>good</u> _____ those you love.

20. Mauricio gets such a <u>kick</u> _____ _____ his little nephew.

21. With our family budget as tight as it is, going on vacation this year is _____ _____ <u>the question.</u>

DISCUSSION

1. In your family, whom do you <u>get along with</u> the best? The worst?

2. What activity do you love to be <u>engaged in</u>? What activity do you hate to be <u>engaged in</u>?

3. When you get home <u>at the end of the day</u>, what is the first thing you do? The second?

4. What things do you really <u>get a kick out of</u>?

5. On your current budget is a vacation possible this year or is it <u>out of the question</u>? Either way, where would you go if you could get away?

REVIEW WEEKS 21-24

WEEK 21

1. I could never run a marathon; _____ best, I can only walk about three miles at a time.

2. I hope you don't mind my stopping in unannounced, but I was _____ the vicinity _____ your apartment and thought it might be fun to visit with you.

3. _____ the circumstances, Paul and Paulette have decided to postpone the gala.

4. When you run to the market, remember to buy milk. We're completely out _____ it.

5. When solicitors call during dinner, Uncle Charlie just hangs _____ _____ them.

6. John has complete disdain _____ anyone who tells lies.

7. Mr. Thompson humiliated that poor student _____ front _____ all of the other students.

8. Biology 220 is _____ far the most difficult course that I have ever taken.

9. The newspaper made an example _____ the man who committed a hate crime.

10. I've often been taken _____ Tom Cruise. Do you see any similarities?

11. It would be nice to see Isabel get _____ the couch and turn off "the tube." She's been sitting there since she lost her job.

12. <u>As a consequence</u> _____ not putting any effort into her work, Peg was fired.

13. I'm so thirsty, but the vending machine is _____ _____ <u>order</u>.

14. Feel free to <u>drop</u> _____ _____ me whenever you're in the neighborhood.

15. That's not true. _____ <u>the contrary</u>, I'm in a fabulous mood!

16. It seems that the economy is <u>falling</u> _____ hard times.

17. A harvest holiday is <u>common</u> _____ many cultures.

18. Yet another basketball player has been <u>accused</u> _____ a violent crime. Why do you think the players are always getting into trouble?

19. The waiter just asked if this "Death By Chocolate" cake was <u>satisfactory</u> _____ me. Is he kidding?

20. Clayton said that his mother had the greatest <u>influence</u> _____ his life.

21. Cathy seems just a little too <u>attached</u> _____ her dog. She won't even go on vacation without him.

WEEK 22

1. Do you think that the death penalty <u>prevents</u> people _____ murdering others?

2. The young employee said that, _____ <u>course</u>, he'd stay late to finish the project.

3. I became a wedding planner completely _____ <u>chance</u> when nobody else was available to organize my baby sister's wedding.

4. The Oscar winner said he was forever <u>grateful</u> _____ the director of the movie.

5. The Olympic athlete was <u>grateful</u> _____ the chance to compete.

6. Mr. Peterson hasn't <u>communicated</u> _____ his siblings in over twenty years.

7. Let's pour lots of water on the campfire so that we make sure we really <u>put</u> it _____ .

8. Leroy thought that the project would take at least three months to finish, but he completed it <u>ahead</u> _____ schedule.

9. Paula <u>dropped</u> _____ _____ college with just one semester to go!

10. I think I left my red sweater at your house. If you <u>stumble</u> _____ it, would you bring it to work tomorrow?

11. Ali knows that he can always <u>count</u> _____ his family to support him in times of crisis.

12. Sy <u>threw</u> _____ his hands in frustration when he couldn't balance his checkbook.

13. Do you think that the department store will <u>take</u> _____ this blouse? It tore to shreds in the washing machine.

14. The rowdy, inebriated students were <u>removed</u> _____ the auditorium when they started heckling the speaker.

15. After a lovely nap, Simon decided it was time to <u>get</u> <u>back</u> _____ work.

16. _____ <u>day</u>, Superman is the mild mannered Clark Kent.

17. <u>Aside</u> _____ the bibliography, Jan has completely finished his term paper.

18. What factors do you think <u>lead</u> _____ Americans being so obese?

19. The junk drawer in my kitchen is filled with things that are <u>useful</u> _____ absolutely nothing.

20. May I have this old milk crate? While it's not <u>useful</u> _____ you, I think I can turn it into a funky coffee table.

21. <u>Hang</u> _____ your hats. The wind is really howling!

WEEK 23

1. The elderly woman <u>leaned</u> _____ her son as she walked into the church.

2. When I bake, I use apple sauce _____ <u>place</u> _____ oil so that my muffins and cookies have less fat.

3. I invited Mr. and Mrs. Morelli, <u>along</u> _____ their children, to our Christmas party.

4. _____ <u>theory</u>, the TV should work once I plug in this wire.

5. Elizabeth Taylor has been <u>divorced</u> _____ at least seven husbands.

6. When you land in Athens, be sure to <u>get</u> _____ <u>touch</u> _____ my family. They'll roll out the red carpet for you.

7. I wish my grandfather would drive a little faster. _____ <u>this</u> <u>rate</u>, we won't get to the movie until it's already started.

8. Do you think that Americans are <u>friendly</u> _____ foreigners?

9. Whatever <u>became</u> _____ Eduardo? He just disappeared from our lives.

10. Did Kelly really <u>ask</u> Alain _____ on a date? What did he say?

11. The teacher bellowed, "Please <u>desist</u> _____ talking in class!"

12. _____ <u>the</u> <u>one</u> hand, Friday evening sounds like the perfect time to get together to work on our final project.

13. _____ <u>the</u> <u>other</u> hand, though, who wants to work on Friday night?

14. After a nasty fight with my sister, I <u>went</u> _____ <u>a walk</u> to cool down.

15. Maria hated living so far <u>away</u> _____ her family. She suffered from terrible homesickness.

16. This class didn't seem hard _____ <u>the</u> <u>beginning</u>, but now it's a killer.

17. The constant parties that my roommates give are a <u>hindrance</u> _____ my studying.

18. Lettie is so <u>critical</u> _____ her mother's cooking. Her mom should just refuse to cook anymore!

19. _____ <u>the</u> <u>whole</u>, this internship has been the best job experience I've ever had.

20. Due to budget cuts, the program is _____ <u>danger</u> _____being closed.

21. Roberto forgot to <u>call</u> _____ when he took a mental health day from work. As a result, he got fired.

WEEK 24

1. Luis tries to <u>get</u> <u>along</u> _____ his cousin Marco, but they just rub each other the wrong way.

2. Did you hear the news? Todd <u>got</u> <u>engaged</u> _____ a girl he met just two weeks ago!

3. Don't interrupt Brian right now. He's very <u>engaged</u> _____ his project.

4. Judy always has to be the center of attention. She'll do just about anything to <u>call</u> <u>attention</u> _____ herself.

5. Do you have any <u>knowledge</u> _____ Victorian literature? I have to write an essay and I really need help.

6. Pablo is trying his first case in court tomorrow, and he is so <u>anxious</u> _____ it that he hasn't slept all week.

7. Look at the sculpture! It's <u>made</u> entirely _____ recycled trash.

8. _____ <u>order</u> _____ achieve his dream of becoming a professional basketball player, Emmet had to practice four hours every day.

9. Joy should never wear shocking pink lipstick. It's really not <u>becoming</u> _____ her.

10. _____ <u>the end</u> _____ <u>the day</u>, Tina is too worn out to do anything but come home, put on her p.j.'s, and watch TV.

11. Joe's boss likes him because he <u>puts</u> _____ a lot of overtime.

12. _____ <u>the moment</u>, Gustavo is too busy to take on any more clients.

13. Let's get to work on this baking and <u>dispense</u> _____ it as soon as possible so that we can head to the beach.

14. I wish that Benjamin would <u>refrain</u> _____ talking in class; he's driving me crazy!

15. When you <u>get back</u> _____ vacation, let's get together to discuss the new semester.

16. Look at that frightened little boy. He's <u>clinging</u> _____ his mother.

17. Unless Fabio <u>apologizes</u> _____ Gabbie, I don't think she'll ever talk to him again.

18. Danielle can't sing a note, but she's amazingly <u>good</u> _____ playing the piano.

19. Grandma always lived by one principle: be <u>good</u> _____ those you love.

20. Mauricio <u>gets</u> such a <u>kick</u> _____ _____ his little nephew.

21. With our family budget as tight as it is, going on vacation this year is _____ _____ <u>the question</u>.

WEEK 25

MONDAY

1. It's almost impossible for me to <u>tell</u> one rap song _____ another.

2. Tony's disdain for this class is <u>apparent</u> _____ everyone in the room.

3. Mr. Wax asked his secretary to find all information <u>pertaining</u> _____ the Lynch trial.

4. Let's walk up to Fifth Avenue. We'll <u>get</u> _____ the trolley there.

5. Finally, the city is _____ <u>the process</u> _____ cleaning up its beaches.

6. Professor Park has the reputation of being <u>lenient</u> _____ his students.

7. What <u>happened</u> _____ Stacey Smythe? Your never hear a word about her anymore.

TUESDAY

1. It's almost impossible for me to <u>tell</u> one rap song _____ another.

2. Tony's disdain for this class is <u>apparent</u> _____ everyone in the room.

3. Mr. Wax asked his secretary to find all information <u>pertaining</u> _____ the Lynch trial.

4. Let's walk up to Fifth Avenue. We'll <u>get</u> _____ the trolley there.

5. Finally, the city is _____ <u>the process</u> _____ cleaning up its beaches.

6. Professor Park has the reputation of being <u>lenient</u> _____ his students.

7. What <u>happened</u> _____ Stacey Smythe? Your never hear a word about her anymore.

8. Juan Cruz is fulfilling a life-long dream and is taking a six month trip _____ <u>sea</u>.

9. Let's drop in on Ellie and try to <u>calm</u> her _____. She's been a nervous wreck since Mark got shipped overseas.

10. _____ <u>present</u>, there are only sixteen students in math class.

11. Sharon <u>used</u> _____ all of the paper in the copier but was too lazy to replace it.

12. This toy specifically states that it is not <u>intended</u> _____ children under three years of age.

13. When troubled, Vanessa always speaks to her grandmother because her grandmother has such profound <u>insights</u> _____ her problems.

14. Why are you <u>fond</u> _____ Carlos? I find him rude and offensive.

WEDNESDAY

1. It's almost impossible for me to <u>tell</u> one rap song _____ another.

2. Tony's disdain for this class is <u>apparent</u> _____ everyone in the room.

3. Mr. Wax asked his secretary to find all information <u>pertaining</u> _____ the Lynch trial.

4. Let's walk up to Fifth Avenue. We'll <u>get</u> _____ the trolley there.

5. Finally, the city is _____ <u>the process</u> _____ cleaning up its beaches.

6. Professor Park has the reputation of being <u>lenient</u> _____ his students.

7. What <u>happened</u> _____ Slacey Smythe? Your never hear a word about her anymore.

8. Juan Cruz is fulfilling a life-long dream and is taking a six month trip _____ <u>sea</u>.

9. Let's drop in on Ellie and try to <u>calm</u> her _____. She's been a nervous wreck since Mark got shipped overseas.

10. _____ <u>present</u>, there are only sixteen students in math class.

11. Sharon <u>used</u> _____ all of the paper in the copier but was too lazy to replace it.

12. This toy specifically states that it is not <u>intended</u> _____ children under three years of age.

13. When troubled, Vanessa always speaks to her grandmother because her grandmother has such profound <u>insights</u> _____ her problems.

14. Why are you <u>fond</u> _____ Carlos? I find him rude and offensive.

15. Who's _____ <u>charge</u> _____ this department? It's very well organized.

16. Do you think there will be individual flying machines _____ <u>the future</u>?

17. Are you sure you don't want to come? _____ <u>that case</u> I'll go without you.

18. Neil promised to be home by ten _____ <u>the latest.</u>

19. We need to <u>collect</u> money _____ everyone in the class if we are going to buy Will a going away present.

20. It took Grace a full month to <u>get</u> _____ the flu.

21. Because Karen is so moody, it's impossible to <u>figure</u> _____ what she really feels about anything.

THURSDAY

1. It's almost impossible for me to <u>tell</u> one rap song _____ another.

2. Tony's disdain for this class is <u>apparent</u> _____ everyone in the room.

3. Mr. Wax asked his secretary to find all information <u>pertaining</u> _____ the Lynch trial.

4. Let's walk up to Fifth Avenue. We'll <u>get</u> _____ the trolley there.

5. Finally, the city is _____ <u>the process</u> _____ cleaning up its beaches.

6. Professor Park has the reputation of being <u>lenient</u> _____ his students.

7. What <u>happened</u> _____ Stacey Smythe? Your never hear a word about her anymore.

8. Juan Cruz is fulfilling a life-long dream and is taking a six month trip _____ <u>sea</u>.

9. Let's drop in on Ellie and try to <u>calm</u> her _____. She's been a nervous wreck since Mark got shipped overseas.

10. _____ <u>present</u>, there are only sixteen students in math class.

11. Sharon <u>used</u> _____ all of the paper in the copier but was too lazy to replace it.

12. This toy specifically states that it is not <u>intended</u> _____ children under three years of age.

13. When troubled, Vanessa always speaks to her grandmother because her grandmother has such profound <u>insights</u> _____ her problems.

14. Why are you <u>fond</u> _____ Carlos? I find him rude and offensive.

15. Who's _____ <u>charge</u> _____ this department? It's very well organized.

16. Do you think there will be individual flying machines _____ <u>the future</u>?

17. Are you sure you don't want to come? _____ <u>that case</u> I'll go without you.

18. Neil promised to be home by ten _____ the <u>latest.</u>

19. We need to <u>collect</u> money _____ everyone in the class if we are going to buy Will a going away present.

20. It took Grace a full month to <u>get</u> _____ the flu.

21. Because Karen is so moody, it's impossible to <u>figure</u> _____ what she really feels about anything.

FRIDAY

1. It's almost impossible for me to <u>tell</u> one rap song _____ another.

2. Tony's disdain for this class is <u>apparent</u> _____ everyone in the room.

3. Mr. Wax asked his secretary to find all information <u>pertaining</u> _____ the Lynch trial.

4. Let's walk up to Fifth Avenue. We'll <u>get</u> _____ the trolley there.

5. Finally, the city is _____ <u>the process</u> _____ cleaning up its beaches.

6. Professor Park has the reputation of being <u>lenient</u> _____ his students.

7. What <u>happened</u> _____ Stacey Smythe? Your never hear a word about her anymore.

8. Juan Cruz is fulfilling a life-long dream and is taking a six month trip _____ <u>sea.</u>

9. Let's drop in on Ellie and try to <u>calm</u> her _____. She's been a nervous wreck since Mark got shipped overseas.

10. _____ <u>present</u>, there are only sixteen students in math class.

11. Sharon <u>used</u> _____ all of the paper in the copier but was too lazy to replace it.

12. This toy specifically states that it is not <u>intended</u> _____ children under three years of age.

13. When troubled, Vanessa always speaks to her grandmother because her grandmother has such profound <u>insights</u> _____ her problems.

14. Why are you <u>fond</u> _____ Carlos? I find him rude and offensive.

15. Who's _____ <u>charge</u> _____ this department? It's very well organized.

16. Do you think there will be individual flying machines _____ <u>the future</u>?

17. Are you sure you don't want to come? _____ <u>that case</u> I'll go without you.

18. Neil promised to be home by ten _____ <u>the latest.</u>

19. We need to <u>collect</u> money _____ everyone in the class if we are going to buy Will a going away present.

20. It took Grace a full month to <u>get</u> _____ the flu.

21. Because Karen is so moody, it's impossible to <u>figure</u> _____ what she really feels about anything.

DISCUSSION

1. Have you <u>figured out</u> what you want to do with your future? What will you be doing in five years? In ten?

2. Do you think parents in this country are too <u>lenient with</u> their children? Do you think they should be stricter? Were you parents strict or lenient?

3. Have you ever had to <u>get over</u> a broken heart? When? Who broke it? How long did it take?

4. <u>At present</u>, what is your favorite possession?

5. When you have "flipped your lid," what is the best way to <u>calm</u> you <u>down</u>?

WEEK 26

MONDAY

1. _____ last, I received the rebate money owed to me by the cereal company. It took three months!

2. We need to recycle newspapers. They are taking _____ all the space in the garage.

3. I always hide my chocolate bars _____ my husband; otherwise, he eats them all.

4. _____ return _____ William's raking the leaves, Mrs. Yantry baked him a delicious apple pie.

5. Emilio had been warned _____ the dangers of hiking without a compass, but he paid no attention until he got lost in the woods.

6. Whenever Mrs. Sheehy needs to go to the doctor, she is dependent _____ one of her children for a ride.

7. In fact, because she doesn't drive, she is dependent on them _____ all of her transportation needs.

TUESDAY

1. _____ last, I received the rebate money owed to me by the cereal company. It took three months!

2. We need to recycle newspapers. They are taking _____ all the space in the garage.

3. I always hide my chocolate bars _____ my husband; otherwise, he eats them all.

4. _____ return _____ William's raking the leaves, Mrs. Yantry baked him a delicious apple pie.

5. Emilio had been <u>warned</u> _____ the dangers of hiking without a compass, but he paid no attention until he got lost in the woods.

6. Whenever Mrs. Sheehy needs to go to the doctor, she is <u>dependent</u> _____ one of her children for a ride.

7. In fact, because she doesn't drive, she is <u>dependent</u> on them _____ all of her transportation needs.

8. I'm so tired of listening to Margarita <u>complain</u> _____ her family. She should speak to them about her unhappiness.

9. _____ the <u>way</u>, I'm going to be an hour late tonight. I hope that isn't going to be a problem.

10. If you get to Yosemite, <u>keep</u> _____ _____ the wild life. The animals look cute but can be very dangerous.

11. Did you <u>grow</u> _____ _____ the city or in the country?

12. The singers encouraged everyone to <u>join</u> _____ when they sang the chorus.

13. Most Republican senators have refused to <u>join</u> _____ the Democrats on this bill.

14. Todd used to be skinny, but during the summer of his junior year, he really <u>filled</u> _____.

WEDNESDAY

1. _____ <u>last</u>, I received the rebate money owed to me by the cereal company. It took three months!

2. We need to recycle newspapers. They are <u>taking</u> _____ all the space in the garage.

3. I always <u>hide</u> my chocolate bars _____ my husband; otherwise, he eats them all.

4. _____ return _____ William's raking the leaves, Mrs. Yantry baked him a delicious apple pie.

5. Emilio had been <u>warned</u> _____ the dangers of hiking without a compass, but he paid no attention until he got lost in the woods.

6. Whenever Mrs. Sheehy needs to go to the doctor, she is <u>dependent</u> _____ one of her children for a ride.

7. In fact, because she doesn't drive, she is <u>dependent</u> on them _____ all of her transportation needs.

8. I'm so tired of listening to Margarita <u>complain</u> _____ her family. She should speak to them about her unhappiness.

9. _____ <u>the way</u>, I'm going to be an hour late tonight. I hope that isn't going to be a problem.

10. If you get to Yosemite, <u>keep</u> _____ _____ the wild life. The animals look cute but can be very dangerous.

11. Did you <u>grow</u> _____ _____ the city or in the country?

12. The singers encouraged everyone to <u>join</u> _____ when they sang the chorus.

13. Most Republican senators have refused to <u>join</u> _____ the Democrats on this bill.

14. Todd used to be skinny, but during the summer of his junior year, he really <u>filled</u> _____.

15. My math teacher told me to rework my paper because she wanted all the work shown _____ <u>detail</u>.

16. They tried to remove the judge from the bench because most people believed that he was <u>unfit</u> _____ office.

17. Why was everyone invited to the picnic <u>except</u> _____ me?

18. When you're at the market, remember to <u>look</u> _____ 1% milk.

19. Take some time when you visit the art museum and really take a <u>look</u> _____ the paintings.

20. Franco needs to be more <u>conscious</u> _____ what words come out of his mouth. Too often, he speaks before he thinks.

21. I don't think I'm going to join you tonight. _____ <u>the</u> <u>moment</u>, I'm just too tired to consider going.

THURSDAY

1. _____ <u>last</u>, I received the rebate money owed to me by the cereal company. It took three months!

2. We need to recycle newspapers. They are <u>taking</u> _____ all the space in the garage.

3. I always <u>hide</u> my chocolate bars _____ my husband; otherwise, he eats them all.

4. _____ <u>return</u> _____ William's raking the leaves, Mrs. Yantry baked him a delicious apple pie.

5. Emilio had been <u>warned</u> _____ the dangers of hiking without a compass, but he paid no attention until he got lost in the woods.

6. Whenever Mrs. Sheehy needs to go to the doctor, she is <u>dependent</u> _____ one of her children for a ride.

7. In fact, because she doesn't drive, she is <u>dependent</u> on them _____ all of her transportation needs.

8. I'm so tired of listening to Margarita <u>complain</u> _____ her family. She should speak to them about her unhappiness.

9. _____ <u>the</u> <u>way</u>, I'm going to be an hour late tonight. I hope that isn't going to be a problem.

10. If you get to Yosemite, <u>keep</u> _____ _____ the wild life. The animals look cute but can be very dangerous.

11. Did you <u>grow</u> _____ _____ the city or in the country?

12. The singers encouraged everyone to <u>join</u> _____ when they sang the chorus.

13. Most Republican senators have refused to join _____ the Democrats on this bill.

14. Todd used to be skinny, but during the summer of his junior year, he really filled _____.

15. My math teacher told me to rework my paper because she wanted all the work shown _____ detail.

16. They tried to remove the judge from the bench because most people believed that he was unfit _____ office.

17. Why was everyone invited to the picnic except _____ me?

18. When you're at the market, remember to look _____ 1% milk.

19. Take some time when you visit the art museum and really take a look _____ the paintings.

20. Franco needs to be more conscious _____ what words come out of his mouth. Too often, he speaks before he thinks.

21. I don't think I'm going to join you tonight. _____ the moment, I'm just too tired to consider going.

FRIDAY

1. _____ last, I received the rebate money owed to me by the cereal company. It took three months!

2. We need to recycle newspapers. They are taking _____ all the space in the garage.

3. I always hide my chocolate bars _____ my husband; otherwise, he eats them all.

4. _____ return _____ William's raking the leaves, Mrs. Yantry baked him a delicious apple pie.

5. Emilio had been warned _____ the dangers of hiking without a compass, but he paid no attention until he got lost in the woods.

6. Whenever Mrs. Sheehy needs to go to the doctor, she is <u>dependent</u> _____ one of her children for a ride.

7. In fact, because she doesn't drive, she is <u>dependent</u> on them _____ all of her transportation needs.

8. I'm so tired of listening to Margarita <u>complain</u> _____ her family. She should speak to them about her unhappiness.

9. _____ the <u>way</u>, I'm going to be an hour late tonight. I hope that isn't going to be a problem.

10. If you get to Yosemite, <u>keep</u> _____ _____ the wild life. The animals look cute but can be very dangerous.

11. Did you <u>grow</u> _____ _____ the city or in the country?

12. The singers encouraged everyone to <u>join</u> _____ when they sang the chorus.

13. Most Republican senators have refused to <u>join</u> _____ the Democrats on this bill.

14. Todd used to be skinny, but during the summer of his junior year, he really <u>filled</u> _____.

15. My math teacher told me to rework my paper because she wanted all the work shown _____ <u>detail</u>.

16. They tried to remove the judge from the bench because most people believed that he was <u>unfit</u> _____ office.

17. Why was everyone invited to the picnic <u>except</u> _____ me?

18. When you're at the market, remember to <u>look</u> _____ 1% milk.

19. Take some time when you visit the art museum and really take a <u>look</u> _____ the paintings.

20. Franco needs to be more <u>conscious</u> _____ what words come out of his mouth. Too often, he speaks before he thinks.

21. I don't think I'm going to join you tonight. _____ the <u>moment</u>, I'm just too tired to consider going.

DISCUSSION

1. Whom do you know who is always complaining? What does he/she complain about?

2. Did you grow up in the city or in the county? Which do you prefer to live in for a period in your life. Which do you think you will prefer when you have a family? When you retire?

3. Do you think the President of the United States is fit or unfit for office? Why?

4. What takes up most of your "free" time? Are these activities you enjoy? What activities would you like to be doing in your free time?

5. How are you feeling at the moment? Describe yourself in detail, including your mood, your health, your fatigue level.

WEEK 27

MONDAY

1. Christmas is a joyous holiday_____ <u>every</u> _____.

2. Terrorism is a <u>menace</u> _____ the entire world.

3. The picnic was canceled <u>due</u> _____ torrential rains.

4. Aunt Suzy is so nosy. She <u>butts</u> _____ everybody's business!

5. The New Year's Eve party was scheduled as an open house, but everyone arrived _____ <u>once.</u>

6. Don't comment on Ben's hair. He's very self-conscious about the fact that it has <u>receded</u> _____ his forehead.

7. In the movie, the bandits successfully <u>got</u> _____ _____ the pursuing posse.

TUESDAY

1. Christmas is a joyous holiday_____ <u>every</u> _____.

2. Terrorism is a <u>menace</u> _____ the entire world.

3. The picnic was canceled <u>due</u> _____ torrential rains.

4. Aunt Suzy is so nosy. She <u>butts</u> _____ everybody's business!

5. The New Year's Eve party was scheduled as an open house, but everyone arrived _____ <u>once.</u>

6. Don't comment on Ben's hair. He's very self-conscious about the fact that it has <u>receded</u> _____ his forehead.

7. In the movie, the bandits successfully <u>got</u> _____ _____ the pursuing posse.

8. Can you stay after class today and help the teacher put _____ the new bulletin boards?

9. Have you heard _____ Betty? She won the lottery and is set for life!

10. Mr. and Mrs. Smith took _____ their nieces after they became orphans.

11. Subsequent _____ Harry's retiring from the law firm, he became an avid gardener.

12. Mr. Jones never caught _____ the fact that the entire class cheated on his exams.

13. The utilities company mistakenly shut _____ my power last night. I spent the entire evening in the dark.

14. It was not love at first sight! _____ first, Nancy and Mario hated each other. It was only much later that they fell passionately in love.

WEDNESDAY

1. Christmas is a joyous holiday_____ every _____.

2. Terrorism is a menace _____ the entire world.

3. The picnic was canceled due _____ torrential rains.

4. Aunt Suzy is so nosy. She butts _____ everybody's business!

5. The New Year's Eve party was scheduled as an open house, but everyone arrived _____ once.

6. Don't comment on Ben's hair. He's very self-conscious about the fact that it has receded _____ his forehead.

7. In the movie, the bandits successfully got _____ _____ the pursuing posse.

8. Can you stay after class today and help the teacher put _____ the new bulletin boards?

9. Have you heard _____ Betty? She won the lottery and is set for life!

10. Mr. and Mrs. Smith took _____ their nieces after they became orphans.

11. Subsequent _____ Harry's retiring from the law firm, he became an avid gardener.

12. Mr. Jones never caught _____ the fact that the entire class cheated on his exams.

13. The utilities company mistakenly shut _____ my power last night. I spent the entire evening in the dark.

14. It was not love at first sight! _____ first, Nancy and Mario hated each other. It was only much later that they fell passionately in love.

15. Marissa loves to show _____. She thinks that whatever she does or whatever she has is absolutely the best.

16. I tried to look _____ Isabel's telephone number in the phone book, but her number is unlisted.

17. Go easy _____ Meredith when you speak to her. She's already so upset about the car accident.

18. Toby is frighteningly adept _____ lying. He can look at you straight in the face and tell you the biggest whopper of a lie.

19. Labor and management united _____ each other to protest the government's intervention in the running of their company.

20. When our favorite TV show went off the air after ten years, I commiserated _____ my friends by watching an all-night marathon of our favorite episodes.

21. The professor decided to require a research paper _____ addition _____ the already scheduled midterm and final.

THURSDAY

1. Christmas is a joyous holiday_____ every _____.

2. Terrorism is a <u>menace</u> _____ the entire world.

3. The picnic was canceled <u>due</u> _____ torrential rains.

4. Aunt Suzy is so nosy. She <u>butts</u> _____ everybody's business!

5. The New Year's Eve party was scheduled as an open house, but everyone arrived _____ <u>once</u>.

6. Don't comment on Ben's hair. He's very self-conscious about the fact that it has <u>receded</u> _____ his forehead.

7. In the movie, the bandits successfully <u>got</u> _____ _____ the pursuing posse.

8. Can you stay after class today and help the teacher <u>put</u> _____ the new bulletin boards?

9. Have you <u>heard</u> _____ Betty? She won the lottery and is set for life!

10. Mr. and Mrs. Smith <u>took</u> _____ their nieces after they became orphans.

11. <u>Subsequent</u> _____ Harry's retiring from the law firm, he became an avid gardener.

12. Mr. Jones never <u>caught</u> _____ the fact that the entire class cheated on his exams.

13. The utilities company mistakenly <u>shut</u> _____ my power last night. I spent the entire evening in the dark.

14. It was not love at first sight! _____ <u>first</u>, Nancy and Mario hated each other. It was only much later that they fell passionately in love.

15. Marissa loves to <u>show</u> _____. She thinks that whatever she does or whatever she has is absolutely the best.

16. I tried to <u>look</u> _____ Isabel's telephone number in the phone book, but her number is unlisted.

17. Go <u>easy</u> _____ Meredith when you speak to her. She's already so upset about the car accident.

18. Toby is frighteningly <u>adept</u> _____ lying. He can look at you straight in the face and tell you the biggest whopper of a lie.

19. Labor and management <u>united</u> _____ each other to protest the government's intervention in the running of their company.

20. When our favorite TV show went off the air after ten years, I <u>commiserated</u> _____ my friends by watching an all-night marathon of our favorite episodes.

21. The professor decided to require a research paper _____ <u>addition</u> _____ the already scheduled midterm and final.

FRIDAY

1. Christmas is a joyous holiday_____ <u>every</u> _____.

2. Terrorism is a <u>menace</u> _____ the entire world.

3. The picnic was canceled <u>due</u> _____ torrential rains.

4. Aunt Suzy is so nosy. She <u>butts</u> _____ everybody's business!

5. The New Year's Eve party was scheduled as an open house, but everyone arrived _____ <u>once.</u>

6. Don't comment on Ben's hair. He's very self-conscious about the fact that it has <u>receded</u> _____ his forehead.

7. In the movie, the bandits successfully <u>got</u> _____ _____ the pursuing posse.

8. Can you stay after class today and help the teacher <u>put</u> _____ the new bulletin boards?

9. Have you <u>heard</u> _____ Betty? She won the lottery and is set for life!

10. Mr. and Mrs. Smith <u>took</u> _____ their nieces after they became orphans.

11. <u>Subsequent</u> _____ Harry's retiring from the law firm, he became an avid gardener.

12. Mr. Jones never <u>caught</u> _____ the fact that the entire class cheated on his exams.

13. The utilities company mistakenly <u>shut</u> _____ my power last night. I spent the entire evening in the dark.

14. It was not love at first sight! _____ <u>first</u>, Nancy and Mario hated each other. It was only much later that they fell passionately in love.

15. Marissa loves to <u>show</u> _____. She thinks that whatever she does or whatever she has is absolutely the best.

16. I tried to <u>look</u> _____ Isabel's telephone number in the phone book, but her number is unlisted.

17. Go <u>easy</u> _____ Meredith when you speak to her. She's already so upset about the car accident.

18. Toby is frighteningly <u>adept</u> _____ lying. He can look at you straight in the face and tell you the biggest whopper of a lie.

19. Labor and management <u>united</u> _____ each other to protest the government's intervention in the running of their company.

20. When our favorite TV show went off the air after ten years, I <u>commiserated</u> _____ my friends by watching an all-night marathon of our favorite episodes.

21. The professor decided to require a research paper _____ <u>addition</u> _____ the already scheduled midterm and final.

DISCUSSION

1. What do you consider to be the greatest <u>menace to</u> world peace?

2. <u>Subsequent to</u> retiring (although this may be many years away), what do you see yourself doing with you life? How old do you think you will be when you retire?

3. Who <u>butts into</u> your life? Do you <u>butt into</u> other people's lives? Whose?

4. Commit to two resolutions, <u>in addition to</u> coming to school to study English every day, that you will follow for the rest of the year.

5. Have you ever become friends with someone whom you disliked <u>at first</u>? Have you ever fallen in love with someone whom you disliked <u>at first</u>?

WEEK 28

MONDAY

1. Janie and Norman went surfing _____ spite _____ the downpour.

2. Did you <u>hear</u> _____ Emile's divorce?

3. What kind of perfume do you <u>have</u> _____? The scent is wonderful.

4. The first thing I do when I get home from work is to <u>change</u> _____ _____ my work clothes.

5. Emma <u>got</u> _____ ceramics to such an extent that she decided to make it her major.

6. Getting some sunlight each day is <u>essential</u> _____ good health.

7. When my daughter <u>came</u> _____ a photograph of me from my college days, she laughed hysterically at my hair style.

TUESDAY

1. Janie and Norman went surfing _____ spite _____ the downpour.

2. Did you <u>hear</u> _____ Emile's divorce?

3. What kind of perfume do you <u>have</u> _____? The scent is wonderful.

4. The first thing I do when I get home from work is to <u>change</u> _____ _____ my work clothes.

5. Emma <u>got</u> _____ ceramics to such an extent that she decided to make it her major.

6. Getting some sunlight each day is <u>essential</u> _____ good health.

7. When my daughter <u>came</u> _____ a photograph of me from my college days, she laughed hysterically at my hair style.

8. Don't forget to <u>give</u> _____ this book when you're finished. It's the only copy I have.

9. Jackie was <u>hesitant</u> _____ going to college away from home, so she went to the local university.

10. Arlene was terribly <u>upset</u> _____ the nasty remarks made behind her back by her supposed best friend.

11. When you finish the application, <u>submit</u> it _____ the receptionist.

12. Usually Valerie likes to stay home at night and cuddle up with a good book; on occasion, however, she is <u>inclined</u> _____ go out dancing.

13. Please <u>excuse</u> me _____ being late to work: my alarm didn't go off.

14. Sandy was <u>excused</u> _____ gym for an entire semester when she broke her ankle.

WEDNESDAY

1. Janie and Norman went surfing _____ spite _____ the downpour.

2. Did you <u>hear</u> _____ Emile's divorce?

3. What kind of perfume do you <u>have</u> _____? The scent is wonderful.

4. The first thing I do when I get home from work is to <u>change</u> _____ _____ my work clothes.

5. Emma <u>got</u> _____ ceramics to such an extent that she decided to make it her major.

6. Getting some sunlight each day is <u>essential</u> _____ good health.

7. When my daughter <u>came</u> _____ a photograph of me from my college days, she laughed hysterically at my hair style.

8. Don't forget to <u>give</u> _____ this book when you're finished. It's the only copy I have.

9. Jackie was <u>hesitant</u> _____ going to college away from home, so she went to the local university.

10. Arlene was terribly <u>upset</u> _____ the nasty remarks made behind her back by her supposed best friend.

11. When you finish the application, <u>submit</u> it _____ the receptionist.

12. Usually Valerie likes to stay home at night and cuddle up with a good book; on occasion, however, she is <u>inclined</u> _____ go out dancing.

13. Please <u>excuse</u> me _____ being late to work: my alarm didn't go off.

14. Sandy was <u>excused</u> _____ gym for an entire semester when she broke her ankle.

15. I'm going to sleep, so would you <u>listen</u> _____ the door and let Dad in when he arrives?

16. I'm not sure that Steve can ever <u>make</u> _____ _____ the terrible way he treated Melanie.

17. Poor Pedro is exhausted. He's working three jobs _____ <u>the same</u> <u>time</u>.

18. Have you <u>talked</u> _____ Charlie lately?

19. I wish my husband were _____ <u>the habit</u> _____ putting his clothes in the hamper instead of leaving them on the floor.

20. Martha is <u>resigned</u> _____ working at the donut shop for as long as it takes for her to finish her degree.

21. Anke is still <u>undecided</u> _____ what profession she wants to pursue after she finishes school.

THURSDAY

1. Janie and Norman went surfing _____ <u>spite</u> _____ the downpour.

2. Did you <u>hear</u> _____ Emile's divorce?

3. What kind of perfume do you <u>have</u> _____? The scent is wonderful.

4. The first thing I do when I get home from work is to <u>change</u> _____ _____ my work clothes.

5. Emma <u>got</u> _____ ceramics to such an extent that she decided to make it her major.

6. Getting some sunlight each day is <u>essential</u> _____ good health.

7. When my daughter <u>came</u> _____ a photograph of me from my college days, she laughed hysterically at my hair style.

8. Don't forget to <u>give</u> _____ this book when you're finished. It's the only copy I have.

9. Jackie was <u>hesitant</u> _____ going to college away from home, so she went to the local university.

10. Arlene was terribly <u>upset</u> _____ the nasty remarks made behind her back by her supposed best friend.

11. When you finish the application, <u>submit</u> it _____ the receptionist.

12. Usually Valerie likes to stay home at night and cuddle up with a good book; on occasion, however, she is <u>inclined</u> _____ go out dancing.

13. Please <u>excuse</u> me _____ being late to work: my alarm didn't go off.

14. Sandy was <u>excused</u> _____ gym for an entire semester when she broke her ankle.

15. I'm going to sleep, so would you <u>listen</u> _____ the door and let Dad in when he arrives?

16. I'm not sure that Steve can ever <u>make</u> _____ _____ the terrible way he treated Melanie.

17. Poor Pedro is exhausted. He's working three jobs _____ <u>the same</u> <u>time</u>.

18. Have you <u>talked</u> _____ Charlie lately?

19. I wish my husband were _____ <u>the</u> <u>habit</u> _____ putting his clothes in the hamper instead of leaving them on the floor.

20. Martha is <u>resigned</u> _____ working at the donut shop for as long as it takes for her to finish her degree.

21. Anke is still <u>undecided</u> _____ what profession she wants to pursue after she finishes school.

FRIDAY

1. Janie and Norman went surfing _____ <u>spite</u> _____ the downpour.

2. Did you <u>hear</u> _____ Emile's divorce?

3. What kind of perfume do you <u>have</u> _____? The scent is wonderful.

4. The first thing I do when I get home from work is to <u>change</u> _____ _____ my work clothes.

5. Emma <u>got</u> _____ ceramics to such an extent that she decided to make it her major.

6. Getting some sunlight each day is <u>essential</u> _____ good health.

7. When my daughter <u>came</u> _____ a photograph of me from my college days, she laughed hysterically at my hair style.

8. Don't forget to give _____ this book when you're finished. It's the only copy I have.

9. Jackie was hesitant _____ going to college away from home, so she went to the local university.

10. Arlene was terribly upset _____ the nasty remarks made behind her back by her supposed best friend.

11. When you finish the application, submit it _____ the receptionist.

12. Usually Valerie likes to stay home at night and cuddle up with a good book; on occasion, however, she is inclined _____ go out dancing.

13. Please excuse me _____ being late to work: my alarm didn't go off.

14. Sandy was excused _____ gym for an entire semester when she broke her ankle.

15. I'm going to sleep, so would you listen _____ the door and let Dad in when he arrives?

16. I'm not sure that Steve can ever make _____ _____ the terrible way he treated Melanie.

17. Poor Pedro is exhausted. He's working three jobs _____ the same time.

18. Have you talked _____ Charlie lately?

19. I wish my husband were _____ the habit _____ putting his clothes in the hamper instead of leaving them on the floor.

20. Martha is resigned _____ working at the donut shop for as long as it takes for her to finish her degree.

21. Anke is still undecided _____ what profession she wants to pursue after she finishes school.

DISCUSSION

1. What hobby would you love to <u>get into</u>?

2. What is the best way for someone to <u>make up for</u> hurting your feelings?

3. What are you <u>in the habit of</u> doing that you know you shouldn't do?

4. Name a change you should make in your daily routine that is <u>essential to</u> your health or to your self-esteem.

5. Name something that your were <u>hesitant about</u> doing that turned out really well.

REVIEW WEEKS 25-28

WEEK 25

1. It's almost impossible for me to <u>tell</u> one rap song _____ another.

2. Tony's disdain for this class is <u>apparent</u> _____ everyone in the room.

3. Mr. Wax asked his secretary to find all information <u>pertaining</u> _____ the Lynch trial.

4. Let's walk up to Fifth Avenue. We'll <u>get</u> _____ the trolley there.

5. Finally, the city is _____ <u>the process</u> _____ cleaning up its beaches.

6. Professor Park has the reputation of being <u>lenient</u> _____ his students.

7. What <u>happened</u> _____ Stacey Smith? Your never hear a word about her anymore.

8. Juan Cruz is fulfilling a life-long dream and is taking a six month trip _____ <u>sea</u>.

9. Let's drop in on Ellie and try to <u>calm</u> her _____. She's been a nervous wreck since Mark got shipped overseas.

10. _____ <u>present</u>, there are only sixteen students in math class.

11. Sharon <u>used</u> _____ all of the paper in the copier but was too lazy to replace it.

12. This toy specifically states that it is not <u>intended</u> _____ children under three years of age.

13. When troubled, Vanessa always speaks to her grandmother because her grandmother has such profound <u>insights</u> _____ her problems.

14. Why are you <u>fond</u> _____ Carlos? I find him rude and offensive.

15. Who's _____ <u>charge</u> _____ this department? It's very well organized.

16. Do you think there will be individual flying machines _____ <u>the future</u>?

17. Are you sure you don't want to come? _____ <u>that case</u> I'll go without you.

18. Neil promised to be home by ten _____ <u>the latest.</u>

19. We need to <u>collect</u> money _____ everyone in the class if we are going to buy Will a going away present.

20. It took Grace a full month to <u>get</u> _____ the flu.

21. Because Karen is so moody, it's impossible to <u>figure</u> _____ what she really feels about anything.

WEEK 26

1. _____ <u>last</u>, I received the rebate money owed to me by the cereal company. It took three months!

2. We need to recycle newspapers. They are <u>taking</u> _____ all the space in the garage.

3. I always <u>hide</u> my chocolate bars _____ my husband; other-wise, he eats them all.

4. _____ <u>return</u> _____ William's raking the leaves, Mrs. Yantry baked him a delicious apple pie.

5. Emilio had been <u>warned</u> _____ the dangers of hiking without a compass, but he paid no attention until he got lost in the woods.

6. Whenever Mrs. Sheehy needs to go to the doctor, she is <u>dependent</u> _____ one of her children for a ride.

7. In fact, because she doesn't drive, she is <u>dependent</u> on them _____ all of her transportation needs.

8. I'm so tired of listening to Margarita <u>complain</u> _____ her family. She should speak to them about her unhappiness.

9. _____ <u>the way</u>, I'm going to be an hour late tonight. I hope that isn't going to be a problem.

10. If you get to Yosemite, <u>keep</u> _____ _____ the wild life. The animals look cute but can be very dangerous.

11. Did you <u>grow</u> _____ _____ the city or in the country?

12. The singers encouraged everyone to <u>join</u> _____ when they sang the chorus.

13. Most Republican senators have refused to <u>join</u> _____ the Democrats on this bill.

14. Todd used to be skinny, but during the summer of his junior year, he really <u>filled</u> _____.

15. My math teacher told me to rework my paper because she wanted all the work shown _____ <u>detail</u>.

16. They tried to remove the judge from the bench because most people believed that he was <u>unfit</u> _____ office.

17. Why was everyone invited to the picnic <u>except</u> _____ me?

18. When you're at the market, remember to <u>look</u> _____ 1% milk.

19. Take some time when you visit the art museum and really take a <u>look</u> _____ the paintings.

20. Franco needs to be more <u>conscious</u> _____ what words come out of his mouth. Too often, he speaks before he thinks.

21. I don't think I'm going to join you tonight. _____ <u>the moment</u>, I'm just too tired to consider going.

WEEK 27

1. Christmas is a joyous holiday_____ <u>every</u> _____.

2. Terrorism is a <u>menace</u> _____ the entire world.

3. The picnic was canceled <u>due</u> _____ torrential rains.

4. Aunt Suzy is so nosy. She <u>butts</u> _____ everybody's business!

5. The New Year's Eve party was scheduled as an open house, but everyone arrived _____ <u>once.</u>

6. Don't comment on Ben's hair. He's very self-conscious about the fact that it has <u>receded</u> _____ his forehead.

7. In the movie, the bandits successfully <u>got</u> _____ _____ the pursuing posse.

8. Can you stay after class today and help the teacher <u>put</u> _____ the new bulletin boards?

9. Have you <u>heard</u> _____ Betty? She won the lottery and is set for life!

10. Mr. and Mrs. Smith <u>took</u> _____ their nieces after they became orphans.

11. <u>Subsequent</u> _____ Harry's retiring from the law firm, he became an avid gardener.

12. Mr. Jones never <u>caught</u> _____ the fact that the entire class cheated on his exams.

13. The utilities company mistakenly <u>shut</u> _____ my power last night. I spent the entire evening in the dark.

14. It was not love at first sight! _____ <u>first</u>, Nancy and Mario hated each other. It was only much later that they fell passionately in love.

15. Marissa loves to <u>show</u> _____. She thinks that whatever she does or whatever she has is absolutely the best.

16. I tried to <u>look</u> _____ Isabel's telephone number in the phone book, but her number is unlisted.

17. Go <u>easy</u> _____ Meredith when you speak to her. She's already so upset about the car accident.

18. Toby is frighteningly <u>adept</u> _____ lying. He can look at you straight in the face and tell you the biggest whopper of a lie.

19. Labor and management <u>united</u> _____ each other to protest the government's intervention in the running of their company.

20. When our favorite TV show went off the air after ten years, I <u>com-miserated</u> _____ my friends by watching an all-night marathon of our favorite episodes.

21. The professor decided to require a research paper _____ <u>addition</u> _____ the already scheduled midterm and final.

WEEK 28

1. Janie and Norman went surfing _____ spite _____ the downpour.

2. Did you <u>hear</u> _____ Emile's divorce?

3. What kind of perfume do you <u>have</u> _____? The scent is wonderful.

4. The first thing I do when I get home from work is to <u>change</u> _____ _____ my work clothes.

5. Emma <u>got</u> _____ ceramics to such an extent that she decided to make it her major.

6. Getting some sunlight each day is <u>essential</u> _____ good health.

7. When my daughter <u>came</u> _____ a photograph of me from my college days, she laughed hysterically at my hair style.

8. Don't forget to <u>give</u> _____ this book when you're finished. It's the only copy I have.

9. Jackie was <u>hesitant</u> _____ going to college away from home, so she went to the local university.

10. Arlene was terribly <u>upset</u> _____ the nasty remarks made behind her back by her supposed best friend.

11. When you finish the application, <u>submit</u> it _____ the receptionist.

12. Usually Valerie likes to stay home at night and cuddle up with a good book; on occasion, however, she is <u>inclined</u> _____ go out dancing.

13. Please <u>excuse</u> me _____ being late to work: my alarm didn't go off.

14. Sandy was <u>excused</u> _____ gym for an entire semester when she broke her ankle.

15. I'm going to sleep, so would you <u>listen</u> _____ the door and let Dad in when he arrives?

16. I'm not sure that Steve can ever <u>make</u> _____ _____ the terrible way he treated Melanie.

17. Poor Pedro is exhausted. He's working three jobs _____ <u>the same</u> <u>time.</u>

18. Have you <u>talked</u> _____ Charlie lately?

19. I wish my husband were _____ <u>the habit</u> _____ putting his clothes in the hamper instead of leaving them on the floor.

20. Martha is <u>resigned</u> _____ working at the donut shop for as long as it takes for her to finish her degree.

21. Anke is still <u>undecided</u> _____ what profession she wants to pursue after she finishes school.

WEEK 29

MONDAY

1. Francesca was instructed to <u>stay</u> _____ _____ the cookie jar because it was too close to dinner. She didn't listen.

2. Coming to adult school has helped Frank become more <u>tolerant</u> _____ people from different cultures.

3. Did you hear that Ross is <u>taking</u> Abby _____ on a date this Friday night?

4. Professor Cox told me that he's very <u>satisfied</u> _____ the progress I've made this term.

5. When you were young, did you ever <u>steal</u> anything _____ a store?

6. Right _____ the <u>beginning</u> I knew that this was going to be a long, boring lecture.

7. I don't know how to <u>extricate</u> myself _____ my credit card debt. I don't know how I accumulated this much debt!

TUESDAY

1. Francesca was instructed to <u>stay</u> _____ _____ the cookie jar because it was too close to dinner. She didn't listen.

2. Coming to adult school has helped Frank become more <u>tolerant</u> _____ people from different cultures.

3. Did you hear that Ross is <u>taking</u> Abby _____ on a date this Friday night?

4. Professor Cox told me that he's very <u>satisfied</u> _____ the progress I've made this term.

5. When you were young, did you ever <u>steal</u> anything _____ a store?

6. Right _____ <u>the</u> <u>beginning</u> I knew that this was going to be a long, boring lecture.

7. I don't know how to <u>extricate</u> myself _____ my credit card debt. I don't know how I accumulated this much debt!

8. Do you <u>cut</u> _____ coupons from the Sunday paper each week? You should. You'll save money.

9. I'll tell you this secret if you promise to <u>keep</u> it _____ Bruce.

10. When Mr. Navato sold his pizzeria, he made a huge <u>profit</u> _____ the sale.

11. Toby threatened to <u>run</u> <u>away</u> _____ home last night, but he only made it to the front door before he changed his mind.

12. I've spent the entire morning in a panic <u>searching</u> _____ my wallet. Have you seen it anywhere?

13. What do you get really <u>irate</u> _____? I get infuriated when people lie to me.

14. When do you <u>get</u> <u>back</u> _____ vacation?

WEDNESDAY

1. Francesca was instructed to <u>stay</u> _____ _____ the cookie jar because it was too close to dinner. She didn't listen.

2. Coming to adult school has helped Frank become more <u>tolerant</u> _____ people from different cultures.

3. Did you hear that Ross is <u>taking</u> Abby _____ on a date this Friday night?

4. Professor Cox told me that he's very <u>satisfied</u> _____ the progress I've made this term.

5. When you were young, did you ever <u>steal</u> anything _____ a store?

6. Right _____ the <u>beginning</u> I knew that this was going to be a long, boring lecture.

7. I don't know how to <u>extricate</u> myself _____ my credit card debt. I don't know how I accumulated this much debt!

8. Do you <u>cut</u> _____ coupons from the Sunday paper each week? You should. You'll save money.

9. I'll tell you this secret if you promise to <u>keep</u> it _____ Bruce.

10. When Mr. Navato sold his pizzeria, he made a huge <u>profit</u> _____ the sale.

11. Toby threatened to <u>run away</u> _____ home last night, but he only made it to the front door before he changed his mind.

12. I've spent the entire morning in a panic <u>searching</u> _____ my wallet. Have you seen it anywhere?

13. What do you get really <u>irate</u> _____? I get infuriated when people lie to me.

14. When do you <u>get back</u> _____ vacation?

15. In a fit of anger, Sara <u>eliminated</u> all pictures of Eric _____ her house.

16. Have you seen Rachel's house? She really <u>goes</u> _____ _____ some weird furniture.

17. Were you <u>named</u> _____ a member of your family?

18. My mother-in-law talks so much that it often takes her 20 minutes to get to the <u>gist</u> _____ her story, and by then nobody is listening!

19. What a <u>perfect</u> day _____ lying in the park and doing absolutely nothing!

20. I hate to <u>infringe</u> _____ your quiet time, but do you think you could help me with my essay? It really needs editing.

21. Thomas is so <u>cynical</u> _____ life that I have a hard time being around him.

THURSDAY

1. Francesca was instructed to <u>stay</u> _____ _____ the cookie jar because it was too close to dinner. She didn't listen.

2. Coming to adult school has helped Frank become more <u>tolerant</u> _____ people from different cultures.

3. Did you hear that Ross is <u>taking</u> Abby _____ on a date this Friday night?

4. Professor Cox told me that he's very <u>satisfied</u> _____ the progress I've made this term.

5. When you were young, did you ever <u>steal</u> anything _____ a store?

6. Right _____ <u>the</u> <u>beginning</u> I knew that this was going to be a long, boring lecture.

7. I don't know how to <u>extricate</u> myself _____ my credit card debt. I don't know how I accumulated this much debt!

8. Do you <u>cut</u> _____ coupons from the Sunday paper each week? You should. You'll save money.

9. I'll tell you this secret if you promise to <u>keep</u> it _____ Bruce.

10. When Mr. Navato sold his pizzeria, he made a huge <u>profit</u> _____ the sale.

11. Toby threatened to <u>run</u> <u>away</u> _____ home last night, but he only made it to the front door before he changed his mind.

12. I've spent the entire morning in a panic <u>searching</u> _____ my wallet. Have you seen it anywhere?

13. What do you get really <u>irate</u> _____? I get infuriated when people lie to me.

14. When do you <u>get</u> <u>back</u> _____ vacation?

15. In a fit of anger, Sara <u>eliminated</u> all pictures of Eric _____ her house.

16. Have you seen Rachel's house? She really <u>goes</u> _____ _____ some weird furniture.

17. Were you <u>named</u> _____ a member of your family?

18. My mother-in-law talks so much that it often takes her 20 minutes to get to the <u>gist</u> _____ her story, and by then nobody is listening!

19. What a <u>perfect</u> day _____ lying in the park and doing absolutely nothing!

20. I hate to <u>infringe</u> _____ your quiet time, but do you think you could help me with my essay? It really needs editing.

21. Thomas is so <u>cynical</u> _____ life that I have a hard time being around him.

FRIDAY

1. Francesca was instructed to <u>stay</u> _____ _____ the cookie jar because it was too close to dinner. She didn't listen.

2. Coming to adult school has helped Frank become more <u>tolerant</u> _____ people from different cultures.

3. Did you hear that Ross is <u>taking</u> Abby _____ on a date this Friday night?

4. Professor Cox told me that he's very <u>satisfied</u> _____ the progress I've made this term.

5. When you were young, did you ever <u>steal</u> anything _____ a store?

6. Right _____ the <u>beginning</u> I knew that this was going to be a long, boring lecture.

7. I don't know how to <u>extricate</u> myself _____ my credit card debt. I don't know how I accumulated this much debt!

8. Do you <u>cut</u> _____ coupons from the Sunday paper each week? You should. You'll save money.

9. I'll tell you this secret if you promise to <u>keep</u> it _____ Bruce.

10. When Mr. Navato sold his pizzeria, he made a huge <u>profit</u> _____ the sale.

11. Toby threatened to <u>run away</u> _____ home last night, but he only made it to the front door before he changed his mind.

12. I've spent the entire morning in a panic <u>searching</u> _____ my wallet. Have you seen it anywhere?

13. What do you get really <u>irate</u> _____? I get infuriated when people lie to me.

14. When do you <u>get back</u> _____ vacation?

15. In a fit of anger, Sara <u>eliminated</u> all pictures of Eric _____ her house.

16. Have you seen Rachel's house? She really <u>goes</u> _____ _____ some weird furniture.

17. Were you <u>named</u> _____ a member of your family?

18. My mother-in-law talks so much that it often takes her 20 minutes to get to the <u>gist</u> _____ her story, and by then nobody is listening!

19. What a <u>perfect</u> day _____ lying in the park and doing absolutely nothing!

20. I hate to <u>infringe</u> _____ your quiet time, but do you think you could help me with my essay? It really needs editing.

21. Thomas is so <u>cynical</u> _____ life that I have a hard time being around him.

DISCUSSION

1. What the most romantic date that you could be <u>taken out on</u>?

2. Were you <u>named for</u> a member of your family? <u>For</u> whom were you <u>named</u>?

3. Are you <u>satisfied with</u> the "track" your life is on? Are you headed in the right direction? Are there any changes you think you should make?

4. Did you ever <u>run away from</u> home when you were a child? Where did you go? What did you bring? What happened?

5. Describe a <u>perfect</u> day <u>for</u> yourself.

WEEK 30

MONDAY

1. Do you think the President is _____ <u>danger</u> _____ being impeached?

2. People shouldn't leave poisonous plants around their houses because there is always the <u>danger</u> _____ a child's chewing on them.

3. Marcy had to cancel her plans for Thursday night. She just wasn't <u>feeling</u> _____ _____ doing anything.

4. Put your finger down! It's not polite to <u>point</u> _____ people.

5. <u>Speaking</u> _____ beautiful places, have you seen Mindy's new home? It's as big as a palace.

6. Joe Green was <u>expelled</u> _____ school last week for smoking in the bathroom. Apparently our school has a zero tolerance policy.

7. Hundreds of teenagers were <u>turned</u> _____ _____ the concert the other night because it was sold out.

TUESDAY

1. Do you think the President is _____ <u>danger</u> _____ being impeached?

2. People shouldn't leave poisonous plants around their houses because there is always the <u>danger</u> _____ a child's chewing on them.

3. Marcy had to cancel her plans for Thursday night. She just wasn't <u>feeling</u> _____ _____ doing anything.

4. Put your finger down! It's not polite to <u>point</u> _____ people.

5. <u>Speaking</u> _____ beautiful places, have you seen Mindy's new home? It's as big as a palace.

6. Joe Green was <u>expelled</u> _____ school last week for smoking in the bathroom. Apparently our school has a zero tolerance policy.

7. Hundreds of teenagers were <u>turned</u> _____ _____ the concert the other night because it was sold out.

8. I spent so much <u>time</u> _____ the final paper. It took me three weeks to research and write it.

9. When Yolanda was <u>looking</u> _____ her father's desk, she found a picture of her parents' wedding day that she hadn't seen before.

10. Because I had <u>qualms</u> _____ marrying Larry, I cancelled the wedding.

11. Tony couldn't be guilty of the crime. _____ <u>the time</u> it was being committed, he was already in jail.

12. Susanna has always <u>struggled</u> _____ mathematics. It just doesn't come easily to her.

13. Last night was wonderful! I <u>turned</u> _____ at 9:00 p.m. and got a great night's sleep.

14. It's sometimes difficult for teenagers to <u>relate</u> _____ the elderly. Their worlds are so far apart.

WEDNESDAY

1. Do you think the President is _____ <u>danger</u> _____ being impeached?

2. People shouldn't leave poisonous plants around their houses because there is always the <u>danger</u> _____ a child's chewing on them.

3. Marcy had to cancel her plans for Thursday night. She just wasn't <u>feeling</u> _____ _____ doing anything.

4. Put your finger down! It's not polite to <u>point</u> _____ people.

5. <u>Speaking</u> _____ beautiful places, have you seen Mindy's new home? It's as big as a palace.

6. Joe Green was <u>expelled</u> _____ school last week for smoking in the bathroom. Apparently our school has a zero tolerance policy.

7. Hundreds of teenagers were <u>turned</u> _____ _____ the concert the other night because it was sold out.

8. I spent so much <u>time</u> _____ the final paper. It took me three weeks to research and write it.

9. When Yolanda was <u>looking</u> _____ her father's desk, she found a picture of her parents' wedding day that she hadn't seen before.

10. Because I had <u>qualms</u> _____ marrying Larry, I cancelled the wedding.

11. Tony couldn't be guilty of the crime. _____ <u>the time</u> it was being committed, he was already in jail.

12. Susanna has always <u>struggled</u> _____ mathematics. It just doesn't come easily to her.

13. Last night was wonderful! I <u>turned</u> _____ at 9:00 p.m. and got a great night's sleep.

14. It's sometimes difficult for teenagers to <u>relate</u> _____ the elderly. Their worlds are so far apart.

15. Supeena had a very hard time <u>adapting</u> _____ the freezing climate of Vermont, so she packed her bags and headed south.

16. John was hired as the CEO of the company _____ <u>the basis</u> _____ his past successes with similar businesses.

17. There is absolutely no <u>evidence</u> _____ arson in San Jose's fire last summer.

18. Dennis felt so <u>left</u> _____ when all of his friends were invited to Toby's party and he was excluded.

19. I cleaned out my closet _____ <u>some</u> <u>extent</u>, but I got hot and tired and decided to finish the project next weekend.

20. Mrs. Jackson was extremely <u>sympathetic</u> _____ me when I asked for time off from work to visit my ailing father.

21. During the summer kids love to be <u>free</u> _____ homework and school.

THURSDAY

1. Do you think the President is _____ <u>danger</u> _____ being impeached?

2. People shouldn't leave poisonous plants around their houses because there is always the <u>danger</u> _____ a child's chewing on them.

3. Marcy had to cancel her plans for Thursday night. She just wasn't <u>feeling</u> _____ _____ doing anything.

4. Put your finger down! It's not polite to <u>point</u> _____ people.

5. <u>Speaking</u> _____ beautiful places, have you seen Mindy's new home? It's as big as a palace.

6. Joe Green was <u>expelled</u> _____ school last week for smoking in the bathroom. Apparently our school has a zero tolerance policy.

7. Hundreds of teenagers were <u>turned</u> _____ _____ the concert the other night because it was sold out.

8. I spent so much <u>time</u> _____ the final paper. It took me three weeks to research and write it.

9. When Yolanda was <u>looking</u> _____ her father's desk, she found a picture of her parents' wedding day that she hadn't seen before.

10. Because I had <u>qualms</u> _____ marrying Larry, I cancelled the wedding.

11. Tony couldn't be guilty of the crime. _____ <u>the</u> <u>time</u> it was being committed, he was already in jail.

12. Susanna has always <u>struggled</u> _____ mathematics. It just doesn't come easily to her.

13. Last night was wonderful! I <u>turned</u> _____ at 9:00 p.m. and got a great night's sleep.

14. It's sometimes difficult for teenagers to <u>relate</u> _____ the elderly. Their worlds are so far apart.

15. Supeena had a very hard time <u>adapting</u> _____ the freezing climate of Vermont, so she packed her bags and headed south.

16. John was hired as the CEO of the company _____ <u>the basis</u> _____ his past successes with similar businesses.

17. There is absolutely no <u>evidence</u> _____ arson in San Jose's fire last summer.

18. Dennis felt so <u>left</u> _____ when all of his friends were invited to Toby's party and he was excluded.

19. I cleaned out my closet _____ <u>some extent</u>, but I got hot and tired and decided to finish the project next weekend.

20. Mrs. Jackson was extremely <u>sympathetic</u> _____ me when I asked for time off from work to visit my ailing father.

21. During the summer kids love to be <u>free</u> _____ homework and school.

FRIDAY

1. Do you think the President is _____ <u>danger</u> _____ being impeached?

2. People shouldn't leave poisonous plants around their houses because there is always the <u>danger</u> _____ a child's chewing on them.

3. Marcy had to cancel her plans for Thursday night. She just wasn't <u>feeling</u> _____ _____ doing anything.

4. Put your finger down! It's not polite to <u>point</u> _____ people.

5. Speaking _____ beautiful places, have you seen Mindy's new home? It's as big as a palace.

6. Joe Green was expelled _____ school last week for smoking in the bathroom. Apparently our school has a zero tolerance policy.

7. Hundreds of teenagers were turned _____ _____ the concert the other night because it was sold out.

8. I spent so much time _____ the final paper. It took me three weeks to research and write it.

9. When Yolanda was looking _____ her father's desk, she found a picture of her parents' wedding day that she hadn't seen before.

10. Because I had qualms _____ marrying Larry, I cancelled the wedding.

11. Tony couldn't be guilty of the crime. _____ the time it was being committed, he was already in jail.

12. Susanna has always struggled _____ mathematics. It just doesn't come easily to her.

13. Last night was wonderful! I turned _____ at 9:00 p.m. and got a great night's sleep.

14. It's sometimes difficult for teenagers to relate _____ the elderly. Their worlds are so far apart.

15. Supeena had a very hard time adapting _____ the freezing climate of Vermont, so she packed her bags and headed south.

16. John was hired as the CEO of the company _____ the basis _____ his past successes with similar businesses.

17. There is absolutely no evidence _____ arson in San Jose's fire last summer.

18. Dennis felt so left _____ when all of his friends were invited to Toby's party and he was excluded.

19. I cleaned out my closet _____ <u>some</u> <u>extent</u>, but I got hot and tired and decided to finish the project next weekend.

20. Mrs. Jackson was extremely <u>sympathetic</u> _____ me when I asked for time off from work to visit my ailing father.

21. During the summer kids love to be <u>free</u> _____ homework and school.

DISCUSSION

1. What do you <u>spend</u> money <u>on</u> that is enjoyable to you? Unenjoyable?

2. Do you think the <u>danger of</u> global warming is real or imagined? If you think it is real, do you think it is imminent? What should we do about it? List three things we should do immediately.

3. When you were in school, which subjects did you <u>struggle with</u>? Which subjects came easily to you?

4. What time do you like to <u>turn in</u> at night? What time did you <u>turn in</u> last night?

5. When you are on vacation, what are you happiest to be <u>free from</u>?

REVIEW WEEKS 29-30

WEEK 29

1. Francesca was instructed to <u>stay</u> _____ _____ the cookie jar because it was too close to dinner. She didn't listen.

2. Coming to adult school has helped Frank become more <u>tolerant</u> _____ people from different cultures.

3. Did you hear that Ross is <u>taking</u> Abby _____ on a date this Friday night?

4. Professor Cox told me that he's very <u>satisfied</u> _____ the progress I've made this term.

5. When you were young, did you ever <u>steal</u> anything _____ a store?

6. Right _____ <u>the</u> <u>beginning</u> I knew that this was going to be a long, boring lecture.

7. I don't know how to <u>extricate</u> myself _____ my credit card debt. I don't know how I accumulated this much debt!

8. Do you <u>cut</u> _____ coupons from the Sunday paper each week? You should. You'll save money.

9. I'll tell you this secret if you promise to <u>keep</u> it _____ Bruce.

10. When Mr. Navato sold his pizzeria, he made a huge <u>profit</u> _____ the sale.

11. Toby threatened to <u>run</u> <u>away</u> _____ home last night, but he only made it to the front door before he changed his mind.

12. I've spent the entire morning in a panic <u>searching</u> _____ my wallet. Have you seen it anywhere?

13. What do you get really <u>irate</u> _____? I get infuriated when people lie to me.

14. When do you <u>get</u> <u>back</u> _____ vacation?

15. In a fit of anger, Sara <u>eliminated</u> all pictures of Eric _____ her house.

16. Have you seen Rachel's house? She really <u>goes</u> _____ some weird furniture.

17. Were you <u>named</u> _____ a member of your family?

18. My mother-in-law talks so much that it often takes her 20 minutes to get to the <u>gist</u> _____ her story, and by then nobody is listening!

19. What a <u>perfect</u> day _____ lying in the park and doing absolutely nothing!

20. I hate to <u>infringe</u> _____ your quiet time, but do you think you could help me with my essay? It really needs editing.

21. Thomas is so <u>cynical</u> _____ life that I have a hard time being around him.

WEEK 30

1. Do you think the President is _____ <u>danger</u> _____ being impeached?

2. People shouldn't leave poisonous plants around their houses because there is always the <u>danger</u> _____ a child's chewing on them.

3. Marcy had to cancel her plans for Thursday night. She just wasn't <u>feeling</u> _____ _____ doing anything.

4. Put your finger down! It's not polite to <u>point</u> _____ people.

5. <u>Speaking</u> _____ beautiful places, have you seen Mindy's new home? It's as big as a palace.

6. Joe Green was <u>expelled</u> _____ school last week for smoking in the bathroom. Apparently our school has a zero tolerance policy.

7. Hundreds of teenagers were <u>turned</u> _____ _____ the concert the other night because it was sold out.

8. I spent so much <u>time</u> _____ the final paper. It took me three weeks to research and write it.

9. When Yolanda was <u>looking</u> _____ her father's desk, she found a picture of her parents' wedding day that she hadn't seen before.

10. Because I had <u>qualms</u> _____ marrying Larry, I cancelled the wedding.

11. Tony couldn't be guilty of the crime. _____ <u>the time</u> it was being committed, he was already in jail.

12. Susanna has always <u>struggled</u> _____ mathematics. It just doesn't come easily to her.

13. Last night was wonderful! I <u>turned</u> _____ at 9:00 p.m. and got a great night's sleep.

14. It's sometimes difficult for teenagers to <u>relate</u> _____ the elderly. Their worlds are so far apart.

15. Supeena had a very hard time <u>adapting</u> _____ the freezing climate of Vermont, so she packed her bags and headed south.

16. John was hired as the CEO of the company _____ <u>the basis</u> _____ his past successes with similar businesses.

17. There is absolutely no <u>evidence</u> _____ arson in San Jose's fire last summer.

18. Dennis felt so <u>left</u> _____ when all of his friends were invited to Toby's party and he was excluded.

19. I cleaned out my closet _____ <u>some extent</u>, but I got hot and tired and decided to finish the project next weekend.

20. Mrs. Jackson was extremely <u>sympathetic</u> _____ me when I asked for time off from work to visit my ailing father.

21. During the summer kids love to be <u>free</u> _____ homework and school.

ANSWER KEY

WEEK 1
1. deviate from 2. abstain from 3. aware of 4. content with 5. provide with 6. thirst for 7. according to 8. envious of 9. at odds with 10. substitute for 11. contribute to, for, toward, towards 12. rescue from 13. care about 14. care for 15. quest for 16. relevant to 17. differ from 18. consult with 19. side with 20. side against 21. detach from

WEEK 2
1. in the event of 2. innocent of 3. on behalf of 4. excels at, in 5. unfamiliar with 6. rely on, upon 7. adjacent to 8. blessed with, by 9. on the advice of 10. homesick for 11. crowded with 12. with the exception of 13. involve in, with 14. yearn for 15. separate from 16. impatient with 17. emerged from 18. deal with 19. distinguish between 20. consist of 21. expert in, at, (on)

WEEK 3
1. devote to 2. in light of 3. responsible for 4. in case of 5. disdain for 6. incapable of 7. incompatible with 8. tired of 9. tired from 10. burdened by, with 11. blame for 12. concerned with, by, about 13. flee from 14. forgive for 15. dissent from 16. polite to 17. demonstrate against, over 18. bored with, by 19. count on, upon 20. zenith of 21. respond to

WEEK 4
1. take advantage of 2. proficient in, at 3. attitude toward, towards, 4. connection between 5. with help from 6. indigenous to 7. annoyed with, at 8. annoyed at, about, by 9. wish for 10. suspicious of 11. quarrel with 12. quarrel over, about 13. photographs of, from 14. on second thought 15. looking back on, at, over 16. object to 17. in the meantime 18. digress from 19. confused with 20. confused by, with, about 21. engrossed in

WEEK 5
1. kind to 2. kind of 3. because of 4. hold up 5. in retrospect 6. result in 7. the result of 8. smile at 9. regardless of 10. possible for 11. plan on 12. once in a while 13. on account of 14. listen to 15. worry about 16. work with 17. account for 18. accustomed to 19. as a result of 20. resigned to 21. take a chance on

WEEK 6
1. doubtful of, about 2. at times 3. in common 4. believe in 5. suitable for, in 6. succumb to 7. for the time being 8. first of all 9. call off 10. borrow from 11. all in all 12. long for 13. use in 14. come to 15. on occasion 16. approve of 17. generous with 18. knock down, over 19. shrink in, from 20. cause of 21. reply to

WEEK 7
1. reason for 2. angry at, with 3. angry about, over 4. associate with 5. similar to 6. turn down 7. in general 8. fed up with 9. catch up with, on 10. overcome with 11. go over, through 12. talk over, about 13. estranged from 14. related to 15. pleasing to 16. interested in 17. belong to 18. affinity for 19. on, in time 20. wonder about 21. different from

WEEK 8
1. cut down on 2. from one day to the next 3. look into, at 4. passed out from 5. afraid of 6.passed away 7. for one thing 8. for another 9. bring about 10. certain of, about 11. enough of 12. argue with 13. argue about, over 14. next to 15. put up with 16. superior to 17. in existence 18. known for 19. qualify for 20. spend on 21. flatter by

WEEK 9
1. look over, at 2. skeptical of 3. curious about 4. famous for 5. decide on, upon 6. prejudiced against 7. in the past 8. intent on, upon 9. by heart 10. waste on 11. confine to 12. out of date 13. carry out 14. after all of 15. convince of 16. maximum of 17. eligible for 18. hope for 19. boast of, about 20. boast to 21. wrestle with

WEEK 10

1. ashamed of 2. show up 3. succeed at 4. escape from 5. turn on, up 6. beware of 7. withdraw from 8. absent from 9. careless about, of, with 10. before long 11. composed of 12. sneer at 13. by hand 14. give into 15. preferable to 16. enthusiastic about 17. detour from 18. jealous of, about 19. on purpose 20. all of a sudden 21. for the most part

WEEK 11

1. in a hurry 2. base on, upon 3. do away with 4. go on and on 5. call on 6. feel sorry for 7. sorry for, about 8. instead of 9. get rid of 10. considerate of 11. watch out for 12. watch for 13. pass for 14. agree on, about 15. agree with 16. hooked on 17. tear down 18. cheer myself up 19. evident from 20. turn in 21. combine with

WEEK 12

1. cross off 2. good of 3. at my worst 4. at my best 5. complain to 6. jeer at 7. by all means 8. in favor of 9. day to day, day by day 10. from time to time 11. do over 12. by mistake 13. in the least 14. look forward to 15. thank for 16. recoil from 17. respect for 18. on, over the radio 19. once and for all 20. pray for 21. allude to

WEEK 13

1. typical of 2. demand from, of 3. oblivious to 4. devoid of 5. in the end 6. suggest to 7. for the first time 8. on top of 9. interfere with 10. remind of 11. in contrast to 12. stand for 13. come from 14. persist in 15. ignorant of, about 16. happy with, about 17. export to 18. import from 19. run into 20. increase from - to 21. detrimental to

WEEK 14

1. adequate for 2. advise of 3. on the way 4. in fact 5. contrary to 6. suspect of 7. encourage by, with 8. put back, away 9. go on without 10. inquire into, about 11. refer to 12. embark on, upon 13. work on 14. opposed to 15. for, with the purpose of 16. tear up 17. get away from 18. attend to 19. get together with 20. take after 21. apologize for

WEEK 15

1. acquaint with 2. keep up with 3. laugh at 4. laugh with 5. epitome of 6. obtain from 7. cover with, by 8. cover for 9. run out of 10. independent of 11. point out 12. retired from 13. clear to 14. in the name of 15. just in, on 16. try on 17. appropriate for 18. tear up 19. faith in 20. look out for 21. vote for

WEEK 16

1.effect on 2. by accident 3. get out of 4. dream of, about 5. compliment on, about 6. get along with 7. gossip about, with 8. prepare for 9. on fire 10. fight for 11. a supply of 12. supply with 13. in a way 14. positive of, about 15. inferior to 16. safe from 17. think (past – thought) of 18. think over, about, of 19. recommend for 20. recommend to 21. delight in

WEEK 17

1. solution to 2. work for 3. good for 4. bring up 5. put off 6. prefer to 7. interrupted by 8. check on, into, out 9. in charge of 10. drop off 11. look on with 12. take from 13. rebel against 14. confidence in 15. pick out 16. on the strength of 17. call for, about 18. get through with 19. get through to 20. in his life 21. detract from

WEEK 18

1. on account of 2. ability in 3. adamant about, in 4. depend on 5. live on 6. excited about, for 7. immune to 8. pleased with, about 9. break into 10. ask for 11. get done with 12. invite to 13. shudder at 14. in the long run 15. for very long 16. turn on, off, up, down 17. turn off, down 18. thrilled by, about, with 19. vulnerable to 20. equal to 21. cooperate with

WEEK 19

1. go ahead of 2. rich in, with 3. force into 4. proud of 5. method of, for 6. apply for 7. apply to 8. loyal to 9. prior to 10. by means of 11. presence of 12. fit into 13. throw away, throw out 14. obligated to, for 15. in lieu of 16. come upon, across 17. proponent of 18. take off 19. in no time (at all) 20. check up on, upon/ check in on, upon 21. disapproves of

WEEK 20
1. equivalent to   2. tendency to   3. take over   4. wait on, upon   5. wait for   6. cost of   7. disappointed in, with, by   8. on the grounds of   9. in contact with   10. full of   11. consent for   12. in many respects   13. necessary for   14. recover from   15. authority on   16. pick up   17. antipathy for, toward   18. faithful to   19. married to   20. access to   21. indebted to

WEEK 21
1. at best   2. in the vicinity of   3. under the circumstances   4. out of   5. hang up on   6. disdain for   7. in front of   8. by far, so far   9. example of   10. take for   11. get off   12. as a consequence of   13. out of order   14. drop in on   15. on, to the contrary   16. fall on   17. common in, to   18. accuse of   19. satisfactory to   20. influence on   21. attach to

WEEK 22
1. prevent from   2. of course   3. by chance   4. grateful to   5. grateful for   6. communicate with   7. put out   8. ahead of   9. drop out of   10. stumble across, upon   11. count on   12. throw up   13. take back   14. remove from   15. get back to   16. by day   17. aside from   18. lead to   19. useful for   20. useful to   21. hang onto

WEEK 23
1. lean on   2. in place of   3. along with   4. in theory   5. divorce from   6. get in touch with   7. at this rate   8. friendly to   9. become of   10. ask out   11. desist from   12. on the one hand   13. on the other hand   14. go for a walk   15. away from   16. in, at the beginning   17. hindrance to   18. critical of   19. on the whole   20. in danger of   21. call in

WEEK 24
1. get along with   2. get engaged to   3. engaged in, with, by   4. call attention to   5. knowledge of   6. anxious about, over   7. made of, from   8. in order to   9. becoming to, on   10. by, at the end of the day   11. put in   12. at, for the moment   13. dispense with   14. refrain from   15. get back from   16. cling to   17. apologize to   18. good at   19. good to   20. kick out of   21. out of the question

WEEK 25

1. tell from   2. apparent to   3. pertain to   4. get on   5. in the process of
6. lenient towards, with   7. happen to   8. at sea   9. calm down   10. at
present   11. use up   12. intend for   13. insight into   14. fond of   15. in
charge of   16. in the future   17. in that case   18. at, by the latest
19. collect from   20. get over   21. figure out

WEEK 26

1. at last   2. take up, over   3. hide from   4. in return for   5. warn of, about
6. dependent on, upon   7. dependent for   8. complain about   9. by
the way   10. keep away from   11. grow up in   12. join in   13. join with
14. fill out   15. in detail   16. unfit for   17. except for   18. look for   19. look
at   20.   conscious of   21. at, for the moment

WEEK 27

1. in every way   2. menace to   3. due to   4. butt into   5. at once
6. recede from 7. get away from 8. put up 9. hear from, about 10. take
in   11. subsequent to   12. catch onto   13. shut off, down   14. at first
15. show off   16. look up, for   17. easy on   18. adept at   19. unite with
20. commiserate with   21. in addition to

WEEK 28

1. in spite of 2. hear about, of 3. have on 4. change out of 5. get into
6. essential to, for 7. come upon, across 8. give back 9. hesitant about
10. upset by, about, over   11. submit to   12. inclined to   13. excuse for
14. excuse from   15. listen for   16. make up for   17. at the same time
18. talk to, with   19. in the habit of   20. resigned to 21. undecided about

WEEK 29

1. stay out of, away from   2. tolerant of   3. take out   4. satisfied with, by
5. steal from   6. in, at, from the beginning   7. extricate from   8. cut out
9. keep from   10. profit from   11. run away from   12. search for 13. irate
about   14. get back from   15. eliminate from   16. go in for   17. name
for, after   18. gist of   19. perfect for   20. infringe on   21. cynical about

WEEK 30

1. in danger of   2. danger of   3. feel up to   4. point at   5. speak of, about   6. expelled from   7. turn away from   8. time on   9. look through   10. qualms about   11. at the time   12. struggle with   13. turn in   14. relate to   15. adapt to   16. on the basis of   17. evidence of   18. left out   19. to some extent   20. sympathetic to   21. free from

Made in the USA
San Bernardino, CA
30 January 2019